NORTH END PAPERS
1618-1880
NEWBURYPORT, MASSACHUSETTS

Development of the North End of the City

by Oliver B. Merrill

Originally published in 1906 & 1908 in
The Newburyport Daily News

Transcribed by Margaret Peckham Motes

CLEARFIELD

Other books by the author

Laurens & Newberry Counties, S.C.: Saluda and Little River Settlement 1749-1775, co-authored with Jesse H. Motes, III. Winner of the National Genealogical Society 1995 Award for Excellence (Methods and Sources.)

South Carolina Memorial: Abstracts of Land Titles – Vol. 1, 1774-1776, co-authored with Jesse H. Motes, III.

Free Blacks and Mulattos in South Carolina – 1850 Census.

Blacks Found in the Deeds of Laurens and Newberry Counties, S.C.: 1785-1827: Listed in Deeds of Gift, Deeds of Sale, Mortgages, Born Free and Freed.

Butcher, Baker, Candlestick Maker and Other Occupations in Newburyport, Massachusetts – 1850 Census.

Irish in South Carolina – 1850 Census.

Migration to South Carolina: Movement from the New England and Mid-Atlantic States – 1850 Census.

Migration to South Carolina – 1850 Census from England, Scotland, Germany, Italy, France, Spain, Russia, Denmark, Sweden, and Switzerland.

Copyright © 2007 by Margaret P. Motes
All Rights Reserved.

Printed for
Clearfield Company by
Genealogical Publishing Co.
Baltimore, Maryland
2007

ISBN-13: 978-0-8063-5323-4
ISBN-10: 0-8063-5323-6

Made in the United States of America

CONTENTS

Foreword..v
Source...vi
Preface..vii
Acknowledgements...ix
No. 1. Some Valuable Articles Being Prepared by O. B .Merrill..............1
No. 2. The Tracy Field and the Houses on It. From 1796 to 1810...........3
No. 3. The Tracy Field and the Houses on It. From 1796 to 1810...........7
No. 4. The Tracy Field and the Houses on It. From 1796 to 1810 12
No. 5. The Field Between Tyng and North Streets. From 1757 to 1851......16
No. 6. Carter's Field..22
No. 7. Archelaus Woodman, Archelaus Adams. From 1618 to 1754..........27
No. 8. North, Tyng, Broad and Carter Streets. From 1796 to 1848..........32
No. 9. Deacon John Kent and His Land. From 1747 to 1812..................37
No. 10. Houses on Kent Field North to Carter Street.
       From 1796 to 1848...42
No. 11. Houses on Warren, Kent and Dove Streets..............................47
No. 12. Industries, 1762 to 1840...53
No. 13. Richard Kent, Senior. 1634 to 1654....................................58
No. 14. Edward Woodman's Land, Kent, High and Monroe Streets
       1681 to 1845..64
No. 15. The Ocean Mill..69
No. 16. Arms, Brush, Hat and Collar Factories, etc.1840 to 1880............75
No. 17. Woodman's Lane and Kent Street 1800 to 1854.....................81
No. 18. The Pioneers—Woodman Farm—Custom House 1650 to 1850....86
No. 19. Merrill and Elm Street 1735 to 1812...................................91
No. 20. Between the Landings 1676 to 1850..................................96
No. 21. Congress to Buck Street 1800 to 1845................................101
No. 22. The Field Between Kent and Buck Street............................105

Obituary of Oliver B. Merrill.. 111

Index...113

Map and Illustrations

1830 Map of Newburyport North End
Fig. 1. View of Belleville area of Newburyport
Fig. 2. Caldwell Distillery
Fig. 3. Brown Manufacturing Company
Fig. 4. Federal home built by Thomas Coker
Fig. 5. "View Near the Laurels"
Fig. 6. Rawson Pilsbury house, High Street
Fig. 7. Market Square circa 1870
Fig. 8. 1876 drawing of the Belleville area
Fig. 9. Panorama of the Belleville area of Newburyport
Fig. 10. Panorama looking north toward Monroe Street
Fig. 11. Looking down Kent Street
Fig. 12. Curtis Hat Factory explosion
Fig. 13. Looking down Green Street
Fig. 14. Foot of Green Street and Merrimac
Fig. 15. Schooners Richard S. Spofford and Horace W. Macomber
Fig. 16. The Macomber with keel
Fig. 17. Old school house on Kent Street
Fig. 18. Albert Currier Block, Monroe Street
Fig. 19. Oliver B. Merrill home, Monroe Street
Fig. 20. Bass-Whitney house, Tyng Street
Fig. 21. 42 Broad Street, built by Thomas Coker
Fig. 22. Benjamin Pilsbury house, Broad Street
Fig. 23. Selfridge home, corner of Eagle and Carter Streets
Fig. 24. Abel Keyes house, Carter Street
Fig. 25. Toppan-Whitney house, High and Kent
Fig. 26. Part of the Ocean Mill built in 1845
Fig. 27. Toppan-Tyng house, High Street

FOREWORD

Arguably the most overlooked and underrated area of Newburyport's history is its North End, whose heritage is perhaps less obvious due to developmental infill that has taken place over the last century. Once large estates of our 17th, 18th and 19th century local gentry overlooked open fields, woodlands and pastures. Ship building enterprises, which produced some of the fastest ships in the world, are today represented by a few extent pilings in the Merrimack River seen only at low tide. Factories once producing rum, fine silverwares, firearms, cotton fabrics and hats have been readapted as housing and medical centers.

The *North End Papers* as published in the Newburyport Daily News in 1906 and 1908 by Oliver Brown Merrill (1836-1912) roughly encompasses an area from Winter to Jefferson Street and High to Merrimac Street including "Belleville," namesake of the Belleville Parish of Newburyport; formally Newbury.

In the years preceding his writing the *North End Papers,* Oliver Merrill, who was living at 35 Monroe Street, was more than aware of the vanishing aspects of his beloved neighborhood. In his twenty-two papers Merrill touches upon events that were nearly forgotten at the turn of the 20th century. Today we look back with gratitude to Merrill for his considerable treasury of hard-to-find facts and stories concerning Newburyport's "North End." The Historical Society of Old Newbury also looks with gratitude to the research of Marge Motes for rediscovering this series and for lovingly transcribing and assembling them for the first time into a single bound volume. Beyond these efforts, Mrs. Motes has both personally photographed and hand selected historic views from the Society's collections to help tell Merrill's story.

Jay Williamson, Curator
Historical Society of Old Newbury, Newburyport, MA

SOURCES

The twenty-two North End Papers written by Oliver B. Merrill, of Newburyport, Massachusetts, were found in the 1906 and 1908 issues of *The Newburyport Daily News*. They appeared weekly. Papers 1 through 16 were published between May 26 and September 8, 1906, and papers 17 through 22 between January 18 and February 29, 1908.

The Newburyport Daily News, Microfilm, Newburyport Public Library, Newburyport, MA

North End Paper No. 18 is from the collection of the Historical Society of Old Newbury. The microfilm copy of the newspaper article was torn and of poor quality to be useful.

Period photographs from the collection of the Historical Society of Old Newbury, Newburyport, MA

Recent photographs were taken by Margaret P. Motes, transcriber.

Newburyport map from the collection of the Historical Society of Old Newbury, Newburyport, MA

Newburyport City Directories, Newburyport Archival Center, Newburyport Public Library, Newburyport, MA

Cover design and map formatted by Raleigh Design, Newburyport, MA

PREFACE

The North End Papers by Oliver B. Merrill were taken from his original work published in 1906 and 1908 in the <u>Newburyport Daily News</u>. All phrasing, spelling, and punctuation are as they appeared in the articles. For example, he never capitalized street as in High street. A bracket [ ] or *sic* has been used to bring to the reader's attention an important correction, missing text or a notation by the transcriber.

These articles concern an important period of Newburyport history for one section of the city—the development of the North End between 1618 and 1888. The articles provide a diversified history across all of the various economic levels in the North End. Merrill lived in the North End at 35 Monroe Street.

O.B. Merrill's primary purpose was to "trace the ownership of the land from the first owners of the soil down to modern time [1908], and to give the history of the substantial and solidly build houses that have stood the sunshine and storms of more than a century, and are good for the use of many generations yet to come." Another important purpose was "to fix the date when the streets above Kent street were opened." In the 1908 articles he made the following addition to his earlier statement: "I am aware that these papers have not been light reading; they were not intended to be such. Their purpose has been to describe for about two centuries, starting from the first owners of the land, a part of our city never before written about. It has cost a great deal of labor, but I shall feel repaid if it has added even a little to the history of one of the most interesting of the old colonial towns. By the courtesy of the [Newburyport Daily] News I have been able to give it to those interested without cost."

"Rod," a unit of measure, is used often throughout these pages. For the benefit of the reader, a rod equals sixteen and one half feet or 5.5 yards. An acre is one chain wide and ten chains long—or ten square chains.

The location of Oliver B. Merrill's working papers for his North End series is unknown.

ACKNOWLEDGEMENTS

This work would not have been completed without the support of numerous people in the Newburyport community, who were interested in seeing the work transcribed and indexed. With their help this publication came together to help understand the changes and development which took place in the North End of Newburyport over two centuries ago.

We should all be thankful to the late Oliver B. Merrill [1836-1912] for the endless hours of research in compiling the information for these articles. Mr. Merrill's love of Newburyport's history and his community has resulted in this current work on the North End Papers being made available again to the people of Newburyport.

I thank my husband, Jesse H. [Skip] Motes, for his continued support on this project and for his assistance; *The Daily News of Newburyport* for their interest in putting together this work from their 1906 and 1908 newspapers. I also to thank Jay Williamson, Curator of the Historical Society of Old Newbury [HSON] for his enthusiasm and help in selecting photographs from their collection and for finding the original newspaper for No. 18 in their collection as the microcopy was of poor quality; and Nancy Thurlow, HSON administrative assistant, for proofreading. I also thank Cody Fraser, HSON volunteer, who works on Newburyport photographs; Cecile Pimental, librarian, Newburyport Archival Research Room, for her love of Newburyport's history and help finding information when problems occurred; Jessica Gill, Archival Services, Newburyport Archival Research Room; Jean Coughlin of Infocus Photographic & Digital Laboratory; and Sarah & John Raleigh of Raleigh Design for the cover design. I also thank the staff of the Information Services, Newburyport Public Library, for keeping me supplied with quarters; Greg Laing, curator, Special Collections, Haverhill Library; Peter Nelson, Amherst College Archives & Special Collections; John Moak, then City Clerk, now Mayor of the City; and Sheila McCoy, administrative assistant, for their help in retrieving information at the Newburyport City Clerk's office; and Lorie Szarek, of Clearfield Publishing Co., for her editorial comments.

Margaret Peckham Motes
Newburyport, MA
July 2006

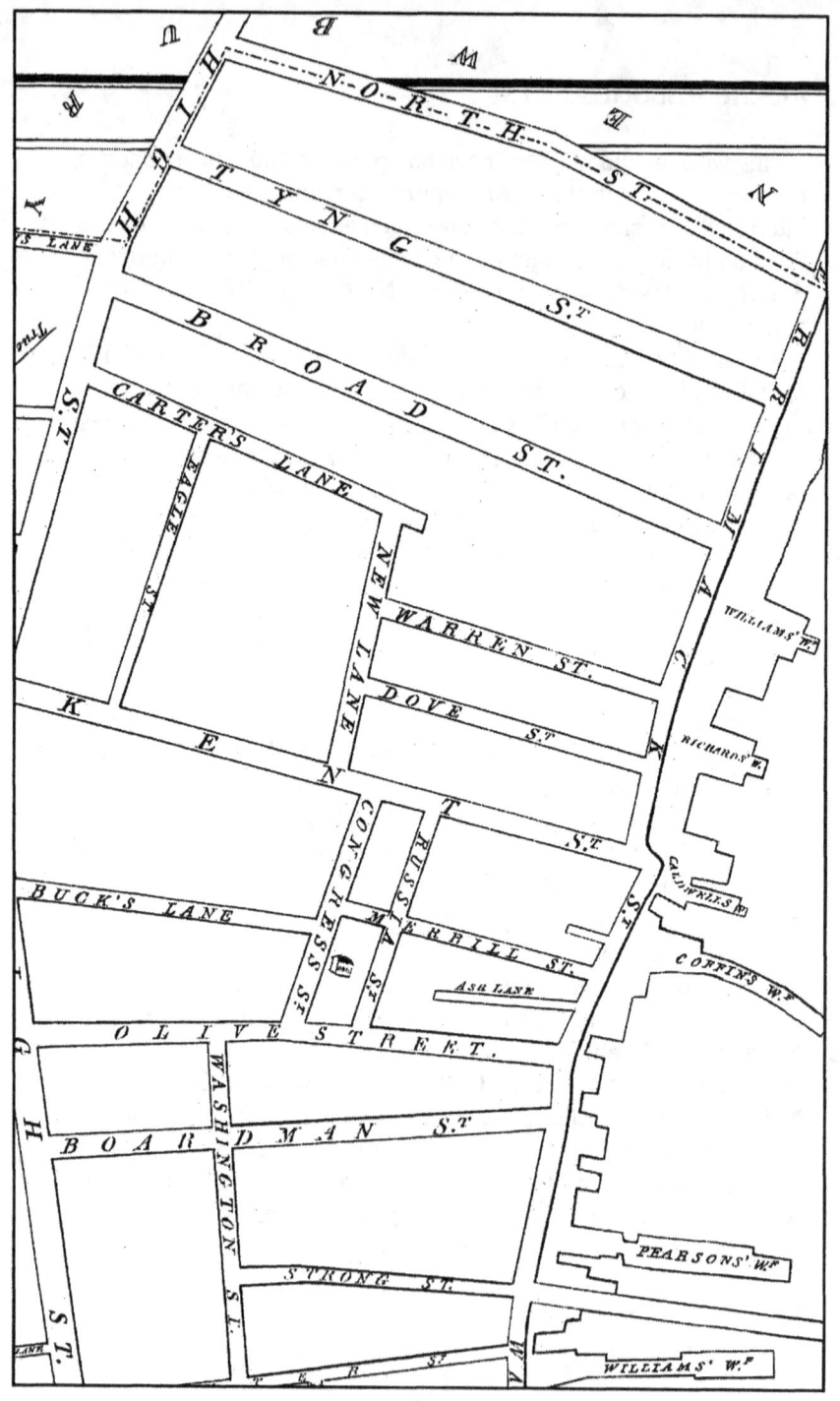

1830 map of Newburyport, surveyed and drawn by Philander Anderson

NORTH END HISTORY

Newburyport Daily News, Wednesday, May 23, 1906

Some Valuable Articles Being Prepared by O.B. Merrill.

Oliver B. Merrill, who has given much of his time lately to historical research, is to write for the *News* a series of articles on the development of the North End of the city. The scope of the work may be appreciated by this resume of what will be treated.

Each story will be completed in itself except for the line of thought running through them all.

The North End means the tract of land bounded by the river, High street, North street, now Oakland, and Woodman lane, now a part of Kent street.

The time covered is from the laying out of the new town of Newbury along the Merrimac River to the time soon after 1840 when a new development started.

The authorities from which the facts to be given have been drawn are the registry of wills and deeds at Salem; the town records of Newbury and Newburyport; files of old newspapers, back to 1792; town histories, books of genealogy and many other sources of information in which our public library abounds.

This old matter that will be presented is, to use a paradox, entirely new. The part of the city above this locality, as well as that below, has been well written up, but this portion has received little attention. As Mr. Merrill has looked up its development he has found it very interesting. If the readers of the *News* find it so Mr. Merrill will feel amply repaid for a year of hard work and that they will so find it goes without saying.

NORTH END PAPERS. NO. 2

Newburyport Daily News, Saturday, May 26, 1906, p 3.

The Tracy Field and the Houses On It.
From 1796 to 1810

The lot of land upon which Thomas built the hospital building was a part of the estate of Patrick Tracy. In 1769 Mr. Tracy bought of John Wood four acres and 74 rods of land for 136£ ($453 1-3). In 1771 he also bought two acres and 72 rods adjoining from the heirs of Archelaus Adams for 59£, 5 shillings ($197 1-2.) This tract of 6 acres and 146 rods extended from the middle of Broad to the middle of Tyng streets, and from High street towards the river down to the bend in the streets, about 100 feet below Monroe street.

Mr. Tracy, in his will, left this land to the children of John Tracy. It could not be sold for money until these children came of age, but could be exchanged for other property of equal value. After the opening of Broad street several lots of land in this field were disposed of in this way, namely two lots on High Street and two on Broad and finally the remainder of the field was bought by Judge Charles Jackson in exchange for a house and 20 acres of land.

Judge Jackson sold his part of nearly five acres to Thomas Thomas for $2000. Thomas at once with Thomas Coker opened Tyng street and sold to Stephen Toppan the lot on the corner of High and Broad streets and the lot on Tyng upon which the three story house stands. This paper will attempt to give a sketch of the houses built upon the Tracy field.

The lot of land on the upper corner of Broad and High streets was bought by Stephen Toppan of Thomas Thomas in 1797. The construction of the house began as early as 1798, but it was not completed for several years. On the assessors book for the year 1800 Mr. Toppan is taxed for this unfinished house $1250. A tradition exists that this house was built and occupied by Captain Frazier, but the registry of deeds shows this is not true, as the transfer of this property is direct from Mr. Toppan to Capt. Jacob Greenleaf in 1805 at the price of $8800.

In 1807 Captain Greenleaf conveyed the property to John Pettingell, the father of his wife, Captain Greenleaf and his wife to have a life interest in it. Captain Greenleaf died in 1837 or '38 and his wife in 1853. In 1854 it became the property of Capt. John H. Spring, a most genial and gentlemanly man whose untimely and accidental death was much deplored. Captain Spring made some changes in the house which to some extent modernized it. He built the porch on the front, placed the balustrade upon the roof and improved it other ways. In 1876 the heirs of Captain Spring sold it to the much respected and beloved Quaker – "Friend" Cartland, and in his life time it was often honored with the presence of the great poet of the Merrimac valley. After the death of Mr. Cartland it passed into the hands of the present owner, A.H. Sawyer.

Thomas Coker was a contractor and builder who constructed many houses both for himself on his own land for sale, but also for other people. He lived in the present lower parish of West Newbury, then a part of Newbury. In 1796 Coker owned a large lot of land of about 220 feet front on Broad street. He divided this into two lots and on the boundary between the lots he dug a well so that half the well went with each lot. Upon these lots he built the two houses now standing there; one a three story, the other a two story house with gambrel roof. In building these two houses on different plans, Coker seems to have been trying an experiment, to see if one of these houses – both equally good would sell in preference to the other. Unfortunately Mr. Coker died in 1804 and did not live to see the results. Perhaps he built the two story one first, and then saw that the big showy three story house was to be the style, and so constructed the other according to the fashion that was gaining ground. The final result was that the three story house sold 10 years before the other and at more than double the price.

It is difficult to fix even approximately the 'genesis' of the three story dwelling houses. Many of them are found in the old towns of New England, but when, how, or where they originated nobody knows. Three story buildings existed that had stores in the first story and rooms for a family in the second and third stories, but these were not the dwelling houses, pure and simple. It is doubtful if any such houses were built in our own town before 1750. Some antiquarians, more familiar than I with older parts of the town may know something about the matter. At the North End no such house was built until some years after 1750, and it is doubtful if any of these houses were built here after 1820. The fashionable styles of house that preceded this were the hipped roof and the gambrel. The hipped roof wasted much room above the second story and the gambrel, especially if dormer windows were put in, involved a good deal of work. The half story which added to the second story made the three story house, was simpler to construct and when built was much more showy and pretentious.

With these houses however the roof was often a source of trouble as it must be nearly flat or without much pitch. The hospital building had at first, it is said, a flat roof tinned, which had to be changed to the one now on it of a considerable pitch.

The rage for building this kind of house was very strong from 1795 to about 1810 or 1812. Few fine houses were built in any other way, which was no doubt a good way for men of wealth, but unfortunately some men of small means were tempted to imitate their richer friends, with the result that many such houses were built but not finished inside, except a room or two. When the hard time came such houses could be bought for less money than the land cost upon which they had been built.

Between 1796 and 1802 or 1803 not less than nine or 10 of these great houses were in process of construction on or near Broad street. At this time three carpenters, contractors and builders, did a flourishing business at the North End, namely Stephen Toppan, Thomas Coker and Moses Coffin.

These men being skilful in their work had many apprentices for whom it was necessary to find employment and they were accustomed to buy house lots and build upon them houses for sale. The services of these skilful mechanics were much in demand, Mr. Toppan especially, built a large number of houses, both for public and private use; he built many of the toll houses and other building of the turnpike corporation, the Newburyport Academy building and a church or two. The houses that Mr. Toppan as well as the other carpenters built for sale upon their own land were probably constructed when their services were not in demand for other people, and when it was desirable to keep the apprentices at work, hence many such houses were several years in building. As much beautiful and elaborate work was done on the interior of these houses, and all by hand, although the workman's day was long and the supply of labor abundant, it was a work, not simply of days as in modern times, but of many months to build these great edifices. Twenty-five of these houses were standing between North and Kent streets 75 years ago, and will be likely to stand unless burned, for a century more.

O. B. MERRILL

NOTE: There was no North End Paper No. 1. The North End series begins with No. 2 which appeared three days after the *North End History*, article of May 23, 1906. M Motes.

NORTH END PAPERS. NO. 3

Newburyport Daily News, Thursday, June 4, 1906, p 5.

The Tracy Field and the Houses On It.
From 1796 to 1810.

The three story house on Broad street, now owned and occupied by Mr. Swasey, as also the two story one below owned and occupied by Mr. Pilbrick, were both built by Thos. Coker between 1796 and 1801. In the Herald for 1801 both these houses were advertised for sale. "Two handsome and convenient dwelling houses on Broad street entirely new with good out buildings and gardens," says the notice.

Mr. Coker died in 1804, and in 1805 his widow sold the three story house to Capt. Moses Goodrich for $3400. Perhaps the fact that Capt. Greenleaf lived in the house above attracted Capt. Goodrich to this house, and their influence brought other veteran ship masters to this locality, for in the course of years nearly twenty of these followers of the sea lived on or near this street. The fact that this was high ground, and commanded a good view of the river and ocean was no doubt one reason for their choice of it for their residence, as here they could aim their long old-fashioned spy glasses at a range limited only by the strength of the lenses.

Capt. Goodrich lived in the house until 1811 and then sold it to Amos Whitmore for $350 [according to Merrill's correction in Paper No. 4, the figure should read $3500.] Mr. Whitmore did not occupy the house and it was probably rented for several years, until 1826 when another sea captain, Henry Southwick, bought it from Whitmore. Many people of middle age remember James Southwick the son of Capt. Southwick, who was a real estate agent in this city thirty years ago, and who was especially interested in the purchase and sale of old-fashioned long clocks.

In 1828 Capt. Southwick sold the house to Mr. Kimball, not a sea captain this time, but a jeweler who manufactured gold beads and other articles of gold and silver. Appearances seem to show that he had a strong box in the cellar of his house in which he kept a stock of the precious metals. Mr. Kimball afterwards opened a store on State street.

In the Herald of May, 1834, is Kimball's advertisement of his new store which was on the lower corner of Pleasant and State streets, previously occupied by Arthur Gilman and in recent years by Mr. Buntin. Here Mr. Kimball sold crockery ware, brittania *sic* and plated ware, watches, jewelry, gold beads and thimbles. He also dealt in "hair work," and many kinds of small industries pertaining to his line of business.

Mr. Kimball's business on State street was not a success. Financial difficulties compelled him in 1834 to assign his property for the benefit of his creditors and the house on Broad street was heavily encumbered. In 1837 the estate being cleared of Kimball's liabilities, was bought by Joseph Akerman for $1750. Here Mr. Akerman lived for more than twenty years.

In 1859 this property again changed hands, being sold to Mr. John R. Spring for $3400. Until this date the house and its surroundings were essentially as when Coker built it, but Mr. Spring made in its outside appearances some very radical changes. He built the broad piazzas that cover nearly three sides of the house. The simple straight doorhead gave place to a porch with fluted columns and Ionic capitals. A balustrade crowned the roof of the house and the old style fence gave place to the heavy one with substantial looking *sic* posts. Had the ghost of Coker come back he would hardly have recognized his three story house.

Mr. Spring for some reason, soon tired of the house, which must have cost him a large sum of money, and in 1862 he sold it to Mr. Wm. H. Swasey who has occupied it more years than any previous owner, and who we trust and hope will enjoy there many more years of a well spent life.

The next house to Mr. Swasey's was built by Coker and as it was not sold at once was rented. It was occupied in 1811 by D.A. White, Esq., afterwards judge of probate. Tradition says that at one time it was the dwelling place of John Pierpoint, lawyer, and afterwards minister of Hollis street church, Boston. Mr. Pierpoint was interested in educational matters and was the author of several valuable school books.

In 1815 this house was bought by Capt. Jacob Brown for $1500 who occupied it until his death. In 1835 we find it advertised to let by Capt. Brown's heirs. Some years afterwards it was occupied by Capt.

Bailey Chace who is remembered by the boys of that period by the fact that when he came home from a voyage he brought with him a barrel of pickled limes, which he sold to the happy purchaser of a big cent at the rate of two for each specimen of Uncle Sam's currency.

In 1849 the house was sold to Joseph Newell of West Newbury, provision dealer, and he in 1855 sold it to Enoch Merrill, dealer in swine. In 1859 it became the property of Rev. Benjamin Hale, retired president of Hobart Free college. Until Dr. Hale bought it, the property was just as when it was built except for wear and tear. Dr. Hale made many additions and alterations in the house which he put in an excellent condition. The improvements made by him were not so expensive or showy as those made at the same time by Mr. Spring, but they were as thorough.

Dr. Hale lived but a few years in the house when death removed him and his heirs in 1864 sold the estate to Mr. Enoch M. Reed, proprietor of the grocery store, now occupied by P.A. Merrill. In 1874 Mr. Reed sold it to A.D. Chandler, agent of the Ocean mill, and from him it passed to the present owner.

The large lot between the house above mentioned and the old hospital building reaching from Broad to Tyng streets was bought of Thomas by Capt. Wm. P. Johnson not for building purposes but for speculation.

Capt. Johnson was a man whose name appears often in public affairs in the closing years of the 18th century. He was a sea captain –a deep sea captain – and so eligible to election to the membership of the Marine society to which venerable institution he was admitted in 1772, and in whose affairs he was prominent until his death in 1804.

After retiring from the sea service he entered upon mercantile pursuits in which he was very successful. His advertisements appear in the old newspapers as merchant, ship broker, etc. While successful, however, as a merchant, his investments in land for himself or his heirs were not encouraging. The land that he bought of Thomas at a high price was advertised repeatedly for sale without a purchaser until 1829 when it was sold to Michael Cressey -- "victitaller" *sic* that is butcher for the sum of $150, about one dollar a rod.

Mr. Cressey built a small house on the Broad street side, and on Tyng street he had buildings where he prepared for market, cattle, sheep and swine, which when turned into beef, mutton and pork, he retailed from his stall in the Market house or delivered to his customers from his covered butcher cart.

In 1832 Joseph Akerman bought the land and buildings and with his brother, Oliver Akerman, conducted an extensive business in the same line as Mr. Cressey.

Mr. Akerman continued his business of butchering here until 1850 when he bought of Moses Toppan a large lot of several acres of land on the corner of Turkey Hill road, once Low street, [according to Mr. Merrill's correction in Paper No. 4 it should read Turkey Hill road and Low street] where he built an immense barn in which he carried on his sanguinary employment and where the swine which lived upon the offal on the animals slaughtered, could revel in their odoriferous feasts without annoying the olfactory senses of the people in general.

After Mr. Akerman removed his slaughter house to Low street, the land was offered for sale, and in 1850 Joseph Akerman sold his part of it, 134 square rods, to Lorenzo Papanti for $980 and in 1854, Oliver Akerman sold his part, about 13 rods with the small house to Lorenzo Papanti for $1000.

The house was moved to Eagle street where it now stands, and in 1855 and 1856 Papanti built the large and beautiful house, now standing there. This when built was the most elegant and costly house of the time. It was one of the first of the new style French roof then coming into fashion and no expense, either in labor or materials, was spared to make of it a mansion. "Signor" Papanti was familiar with the beautiful buildings of Florence and other noted cities of Europe and wished his new house to equal them. Here he spent each summer, with his horses, and his hunting dogs, and the crack of his double barreled gun was often heard on the sea shore and in the swamps. After his death it was for sale for a considerable time. Mr. Stephen Green, agent of the Whitefield mills, occupied it a few years and then it was sold to its present owner.

The lot which now forms the corner of Broad and Monroe streets was sold in 1797 by Thomas to Joseph Edwards, distiller, and his heirs sold to the late Emory Coffin. In 1818 the town bought of Mr. Coffin the lot upon which the school house and bell tower now stand. The school house was used for a primary school about 25 years, then for a volunteer engine company named "The Warren Currier", afterwards for the parochial school and now is used as the Amenian *sic* chapel. The remainder of the Edwards lot was sold to Geo. Currier who built the brick house, now there, about 1850.

The next lot which was the last in the Tracy field was bought of Thomas Coker by Moses and Nathan Coffin who intended to build on it a double house. Moses Coffin built his half and left the southwest side so that Nathan's part could be joined to it, but soon afterwards the development of the great Northwestern territory began to attract immigrants and the rich land of the Ohio called way from New England many settlers. Nathan Coffin was one of them thus anticipating by his act the advice given many years later by Horace Greeley.

Mr. Coffin occupied the house during the active part of his life, and after his death, it was sold to Theophilus Bradbury. Some changes were made in the roof and a few minor alterations but in general the outside of the house is much as the old time carpenters finished it. It is the only one of the houses on Broad street in which the neat and graceful finish about the front door remains—Pilasters on the sides supporting a neat gable – within which is a half circle containing a fan light. Very few of the houses of a century ago retain the attractive finish about the front entrances, as this part of the house seems to be the first that the modernizer attacks.

The Coffin house was occupied for several years by Mr. Papinti *sic,* before his new home was built. The large lot on the lower side of Monroe street reaching from Broad to Carter streets was then vacant and this was rented by him and upon it was placed temporary buildings for his horses and dogs. It was happiness for him to be rigged out in a hunting suit, and with Joe Crafts, the best known nimrod of his time, by his side, in an old covered wagon, with the dogs in the rear, the guns by his side, and a hamper under the seat to go forth in quest of game.

This North End paper completes the sketch of the houses on Broad street in the Tracy field. The next paper will complete the account of the houses on the remainder of this field upon Tyng and High streets.
O.B. MERRILL

NOTE: Mr. Merrill made the following correction in the North End paper No. 4. Stating that "Turkey Hill road, once Low street should read "and" instead of once. Also $350 should be $3500.

NORTH END PAPERS. NO. 4

Newburyport Daily News, Saturday, June 16, 1906, p 5.

The Tracy Field and the Houses On It.
From 1796 to 1810.

In 1796 Abner Toppan, brother of Stephen, bought of the Tracy estate in exchange for property of equal value, the lot on High street upon which he built the house now there, probably about 1796. An advertisement in the Herald of December, 1797, announces that Abner Toppan had removed his shop to High street, near the corner of Broad street, where he continues the "cabinet making business." Here my old ledger shows, he made bedsteads, tables, chairs, book cases, cabinets and cradles as well as doors and sashes.

This shop stood on the south east side of the house and after Mr. Toppan's death was occupied by that very ingenious mechanic, Charles R. Sargent. This building was finally removed to Walnut street and converted into a dwelling house.

Mr. Toppan died in 1836 or '37 and in 1837 the house was sold to Nathan Blake who with the late Wm. Colman conducted for many years a successful business as dealers in meat and provisions. After the death of Mr. Blake the property was bought by the late Paul Titcomb in 1872. In front of this house is an old tree which is now becoming rare –the old fashioned catalpa – which blooms late but for a short time is beautiful with a mass of delicate blossoms.

The lot on the lower corner of High and Tyng street was bought of the Tracy estate in the same way that Abner Toppan bought his, and upon it in 1796 or '97 Jeremiah Sawyer built the house now standing there. This house with dormer windows in the gambrel roof and a piazza in front was intended for a more costly house than Mr. Toppan's. The price for which it was sold in 1799 seems to indicate its value for in that year it was bought by John Goodwin, a wealthy merchant of 800f *sic* ($2666 2-3). Goodwin occupied it until 1808 and then sold it to Luther Waterman, a merchant who did a large business in the buildings between State and Inn streets on Market

Square. An interesting description of this great store is found in Miss Emery's "Nonagenarian."

The price paid by Waterman for the house was $4000.

In 1840 the estate was sold to Richard W. Drown, the jeweler, whose store stood next below the landing at the foot of Green street. In 1845 Mr. Drown moved to the house on the lower corner of High and Court streets, and he sold the house on High street to Ebenezer Stedman. Mr. Stedman's advertisement is found in the Herald from the early years of the 19th century. His store was on the south side of Market square probably in the store where Mr. Graham now sells meat, which fifty years ago was occupied by A.A. Call as a bookstore. Here Mr. Stedman kept many things now sold in a bookstore, and many kinds of merchandise that are unknown to the book trade. He sold Bibles of all kinds; the American Preceptor, Morse's Geography; books in divinity, law and physics; quills, wafers, ink powders, quadrants, barometers, thermometers, umbrellas, walking sticks, fans, beaver hats, jewelry, and some times garden seeds, grape vines, and mulberry trees.

Mr. Stedman's was not the only book store in Market square, Angier Marsh sold books and charts; Thomas & Whipple sold books and various other things, one of their books was the harrowing tale of "Obi, the Three Fingered Jack." The sign in front of their store was "Johnson's Head". Whether this was a picture or a carving, whether it represented Dr. Johnson who compiled the dictionary or "Rare Ben Jonson"*sic* the advertisement does not say.

In 1849 Jacob M. Pierce bought the property, and in 1865 it passed to Richard W. Moulton and from him to Jacob A. Balch who in 1872 sold it to Richard Stone, for many years treasurer of the Institution for Savings. The lot on Tyng street next below the house just mentioned was bought of Thomas in 1797, by Stephen Toppan, 51 rods for $412. In 1807 Mr. Toppan sold the lot to Humphrey Webster who erected the three-story house now there, but did not finish it. About 1812 Webster bought the large tract of land on the corner of Woodland and High streets, and on this built the three-story house recently occupied by Geo. L. Jackman. About 1855 or '56 Geo. W. Jackman bought the field that Webster owned in 1812, and built on it his mansion which with its fine garden, became an attractive feature of the North End. The Tyng street house was mortgaged in 1816 to John Buswell and in 1827 the property was sold to foreclose the mortgage. It was bought by Joseph Babson, 3rd, for $210, about half the cost of the land upon which it was built. At this time it was difficult to sell real estate at any price and this was not the only estate that was sold "for a song."

Mr. Babson died in 1829 and in 1833 the administrator of his estate sold the property to Jeremiah Carter for $625. Mr. Carter established here a slaughterhouse and transacted a large business in meat of various kinds. He had a stall in the Market house, and his white topped butcher cart did a thriving trade from house to house. Mr. Carter was a very pleasant and genial man, and was popular with his large number of customers. He was especially popular with the boys and allowed them free access to his premises where a struggle often took place between a refractory steer and the attendant with the long handled hammer. After the Papanti house was built Mr. Carter sold a part of land to Papanti and in 1857 the house was sold to Ellphalet Griffin, Esq. Mr. Griffin made repairs and alterations which made of it a very commodious dwelling where he resided until he built his handsome house on High street. In 1868 the property was bought by John M. Bradbury, Esq.

The three-story house now occupied by Herbert Patten was built by Joseph Babson, Jr. in 1805. In 1798 Benjamin Choate bought the lot of Thomas and in 1805 he sold it to Mr. Babson. Mr. Babson was a painter and from 1800 to 1829 did a large business. His ledger in my possession contains accounts with many of the principal mechanics and ship owners of the time, and gives a clue to the time when some of the North End houses were built.

The house built by him was kept by his heirs until 1872 when it passed into the hands of Mr. Wm. Tucker, who spent much time and money in modernizing it. The small house above the Babson house was made from the barn that once stood in the rear of the Babson house, and was moved out to the street, and put in its present condition by Mr. Tucker.

The cottage house on the corner of Tyng and Monroe streets was built by Robert M. Merrill in 1846, and was sold to the present owner in 1892. This was the first house built on any part of Monroe street.

This concludes the sketch of the Tracy field. The value of this land in 1770 was $650.87; in 1796 with no house on it $3000; in 1810 with nine houses about $25,000, and in 1904 with thirteen houses not far from $40,000. No one of the thirteen houses is now owned or occupied by a descendant of the first owner, and in no one of these houses is any one now living who lived there in 1860.

The next North End paper will give a sketch of the land and houses from the Middle of Tyng to the middle of North streets, which was the extent in that direction of the great field of twenty acres belonging to the homestead of Archelaus Adams of which the Tracy field was also a part.

O. B. MERRILL

Errata. – Turkey Hill road once Low street should read "and" instead of once. Also $350 should be $3500. – O.B.M.

NORTH END PAPERS. NO. 5

Newburyport Daily News, Saturday, June 23, 1906, p 5.

The Field Between Tyng and North Streets
From 1757 to 1851.

  The middle of Tyng street was the dividing line between the Tracy field and the land owned in 1796 by Thomas Coker. This land like the Tracy field was a part of the "homestead" of Archelaus Adams and was bought of John, son of Archelaus Adams by Samuel Coker of West Newbury. It measured three acres and cost 40£ ($133 1-3). It extended about half way from Tyng street to North street, and down the street as far as the Tracy field extended. Coker bought this in 1757. In 1764 the remainder of the field, measuring two acres and seven rods, was sold to John Woods for 40£ ($133 1-3). The northwest boundary of this lot was the middle of North street, which was also the boundary of the 20 acres that was part of the estate of Archelaus Adams.

  Thomas Coker was the son of Samuel, and from him received the land that he owned in 1796. The lot farthest down the street on Coker's land was the one upon which stands the large three story house now owned and occupied by James Whitney. This lot was bought and the house built in 1807 by Edward Bass, Jr., nephew of Bishop Bass. Soon after Mr. Bass began construction of this house which he evidently meant for a home, misfortune overtook him in the death of his wife and infant son. The house was several years in building and was never occupied by its owner. In the course of time it was finished and was rented until about 1858.

  Mr. Bass was a painter by trade and in his day was successful both as a skillful mechanic and a careful business man. His place of business was the brick store on Merrimac street now occupied by John Casey, grocer and his residence in which he lived and where he died, was the house adjoining the lower side of his store. This house was burned some years ago and a new one built in its place.

  Mr. Bass died soon after 1840 and his only son Edward inherited his property. Edward was a jeweler and had his shop in a room in the second story of the brick building, where he did a considerable business in repairing jewelry. Mr. Bass was modest and retiring but very intelligent. He was a great reader and accumulated quite a collection of old fashioned books and magazines which furnished entertainment for many readers before the establishment of the public library. Mr. Bass died in 1851 [according to Merrill's correction in Paper No. 7 Mr. Bass died in 1858] and his estate went by inheritance to Mr. Whitney, his cousin.

The house on Tyng street is a fine specimen of the architecture and workmanship of a century ago. The porch in front is a more recent addition but it is in keeping with the style of the house, being of the kind that the builder would have placed there. A noticeable feature of this house is the finish of the front entrance which is of the same form as that about the doors of the brick block on Brown square which was built in 1810. Sidelights reaching half the length of the doorway, an elliptical arch with fan light and a door of six panels with an iron knocker.

The house next above Mr. Whitney's the residence of P.A. Merrill, was built n 1865 by the late Daniel Bridges upon a part of the lot originally owned by Mr. Bass. The Cheney house in which Captain Wm. A. Cheney passed many years of his life was probably built by Moses Coffin, who bought the land of Coker, and in 1808 sold the house and 21 rods of land to Moody Heath for $315. The house was small, only four rooms, which accounts for the low price paid for it.

In 1811 it was sold to two persons, Amos Skeels buying one-half and James Merrill the other, the division line running though the middle of the front entry. Skeels paid $300 for his half and in 1817 he bought Merrill's part for $200. Mr. Skeels was a distiller by trade when he purchased this house, but afterward became a soap boiler. His place of business was on the wharf nearly opposite the foot of Boardman street, and his wagon was often to be seen on the streets. He collected wood ashes and grease of all sorts. The wood ashes when leached gave a solution of potash and the grease when "tried out" furnished fat, while the chemical union of the two resulted in the old-fashioned soft soap. That the odors from the works rivaled those of cologne, needes *sic* little proof.

In 1821 Skeels sold the whole house to William A. Cheney for $300. In 1828 Cheney bought of Waterhouse the land below and in 1829 a large lot of 70 rods above his house. He also built the addition to the rear of the house and the barn.

Captain Cheney retired from sea service about 1850 and until disabled by blindness, took much pride in the condition of his house. Every autumn the blinds were taken off and housed for the winter; the fences received each spring a brilliant coat of white wash and the same watchful care was spent upon his house that he had exercised upon his vessel.

Captain Cheney's garden contained the first gravenstein apple tree set out in this part of the "North End" and under his barn was built the first "filtered" brick cistern here, the waters of which the neighbors were kindly invited to compare with the contents of their rain water hogsheads. Captain Cheney died in 1876, a respected citizen and a kindly neighbor.

Monroe street from Tyng to North was opened in 1848. At this time the only house on the "block" bounded by High, North, Monroe and Tyng was the one now owned and occupied by Rev. Dr. Emery. The first house built was on the corner of Tyng and Monroe street by Mr. Adams of New Hampshire on the lot bought of Captain Cheney, who in 1829 had bought of the estate of Joseph Babson 70 rods of land, including the part through which the new street passed. Cheney paid for this land one dollar a rod in 1829; he sold it for $15 a rod. Babson bought the land of Converse Francis in 1822 for $1.60 a rod, being the lot that Francis bought of Joshua Morse in 1819 and that Morse received from the Coker estate. Adams sold the house to David Edgerly, by whose daughter it is now owned.

The house next above on Monroe street was built by Pottle Richardson, and the small house on the corner of North street was moved there. Soon after the new street was opened this pleasant corner was disgraced by two wretched old buildings moved there by the owner of the land, who was not a citizen of Newburyport. To do evil that good may come is theoretically wicked, but sometimes practically – to be winked at – and when the torch of the incendiary removed these buildings nobody felt bad.

The cottage house now owned by Daniel Quill was built by Mr. O'Neil, the double tenement next above by James Blood; the small house next by Mr. York, an employee in the Ocean mill. These were all built within a few years after 1848. The house below Parochial School house was built on Carter street by Seth, Babson and Wm. Teel, who for several years used it as a sash and blind factory. It was sold to the late John B. Lord, moved to its present location and converted into a dwelling house. The Parochial school building is the most recent erection upon the whole block.

The house on the corner of High was built by the late Elder D.P. Pike for his son Benjamin, who was the successor to Henry W. Chapman as master of the boys grammar school on Forrester street in 1870. The group of four modern houses on Tyng street were built in 1888 upon land that had belonged to Mr. Papanti. Signor Papanti began to invest a part of the fortune that his nimble heels had brought him in land at the North End about 1850. He bought the large field on the supper side of North street known as Thomas Emery's farm, as well as land on Carter street and the lot mentioned above. His investment in houses and land amounted to a small fortune, but after his death his heirs were glad to sell at a fraction of the cost.

The house above the four mentioned was built by A.S. Flanders, the well known junk dealer, in 1866. Mr. Flanders came here soon after 1840 and began business as a peddler of tin ware. People whose memory goes back a half century or more, to the younger days of Mr. Flanders, will remember him as a very pleasant and attractive man. He was a fine personal appearance, gentlemanly in behavior, bright and intelligent and a good business man. His peddler's cart painted bright green was kept clean and shining, and the spirited grey horse that drew it was greatly admired. With pleasing manner and kindly ways he was for some years the prince of peddlers.

The house on the lower corner of Monroe and North street as well as the two below it are modern and built there within a few years. The gambrel roof house on the corner of High and Tyng streets is evidently some years older than the houses already described. The land was bought in 1757 by Sam Coker, bounded west by the country road. The price paid for it shows that no house was on it then. No deed is on record that shows any transfer of it to any one until 1809 when it was sold by the widow of Thomas Coker to Amos Atkinson. The inference is that either Thomas Coker or his father built the house. In 1796 it was occupied by Thomas Emery, who soon after built the three story house on the corner of High and North streets. In 1827 it was sold to Flavins Emery, father of Rev. Dr. Emery and has remained in his family ever since.

This house is an excellent type of the style that prevailed from the beginning to nearly the close of the 18th century. Thanks to the present owner the hand of the modernizer had been kept away from its exterior, and we are able to see it as it looked probably 125 years ago. The features of this house worthy of notice are the finish about the outside doors; over the front the old-fashioned gabled finish, a style which can be traced back more than 200 years and which was placed on houses much older than the gambrel roof, and the porch on the end of the house. The pattern of the porch on this kind of house was nearly always the same, that is a gable in front of varying size and finish and with a window on each side. A good specimen of this style is seen on the "George" house on Washington street.

A paragraph in the Herald of Feb. 16, 1871, says that Stephen Toppan's residence on Toppan's land – now occupied by Edward Little, was built in 1785, and the one on the corner where Mr. Dodge's house stands in 1787. The erection of these houses at this time may have led to the building of this house by Thomas Coker. There is no doubt that when this was built there was no other house upon any part of the 20 acres that was a part of the "homestead" of Archelaus Adams.

The land between Coker's and the middle of North street was not used for building purposes until after 1848. It was divided into small lots and changed owners several times between 1764 and 1848, but no house was erected upon any part of it until after 1848.

The house opposite the head of Tyng street, although not built on the land of Archelaus Adams and not within the bounds of old Newburyport, is worthy of notice as a part of the neighborhood. The boundary line between the towns came up Toppan's lane to the upper corner of High street. Here a large stone post stood near Mr. Colman's house. From this terminal the line struck diagonally across High street to the middle of North street to another stone post which born on the upper side a capital "N" and on the lower side "N.P." thus Mr. Colman's house and the three houses above on High street, were in Newbury.

The three story house in question was built by Stephen Toppan upon his own land and sold in 1799 to Dudley A. Tyng for £800 ($2666 2-3). In 1804 Tyng sold it to Nathaniel Smith for $3600, and in 1810 Smith sold it to Captain Reuben Jones for $4000. Captain Jones lived here until his death and his widow continued to occupy it until her death in 1855, when D.A. Tyng bought and sold it to Dr. Job T. Dickens, who modernized it to some extent. In 1865 it passed into the possession of John D. Pike and after him to Dudley Tilton, Esq.

The value of the tract of land between Tyng and North streets is approximately as follows: In 1764 about $300; in 1796, if estimated at the value put on it by speculators about $10,000; if by its actual value as an investment not more than $3000; in 1905 with 22 houses not far from $40,000.

North End paper No. 6 will complete the sketch of the 20 acres that was part of the homestead of Archelaus Adams and paper No. 7 will give what can be found about Archelaus Adams and his grandfather, Archalaus Woodman, thus carrying the sketch back to about 1650.
O.B. MERRILL

NOTE: O.B. Merrill made the following correction to the North End Papers No. 5 in the North End Papers No. 7 of July 7, 1906: "Addenda—In North End papers No. 5, the date of the death of Edward Bass should have been 1858 instead of 1851."

NORTH END PAPERS—NO. 6
[According to a correction by Merrill's North End Papers No. 7, the subject was Carter's Field and the number is No. 6, not 5 as published.]

Newburyport Daily News, Saturday, June 30, 1906, p 5.

Carter's Field
[According to Merrill's correction in Paper No. 7. The Field Between Tyng and North Street should read Carter's Field]

Among the men prominent in local public affairs, not only in old Newbury, but in Newburyport, the name of Nathaniel Carter was prominent. His long life of 86 years covered a large part of the 18th century, closing in 1828.

Mr. Carter was one of the foremost in urging the movement of separation from the mother town, as he saw clearly that the diversity of interests between the farming and the mercantile parts would never be made to harmonize. He was active in urging the move for separation which for political reasons met with much opposition from the "great and general court."

After the incorporation of Newburyport he was the first treasurer, a new office, as the old town had entrusted that duty to the selectmen – an arrangement which was not at all satisfactory to the mercantile population, which paid a large part of taxes levied for town expenses. One of the first interests provided for by the new town was the educational. A committee of five men was chosen to provide accommodations for two writing schools and the Latin grammar school, for boys, of course, the girls having to wait almost thirty years for the appointment of the "four discreet school dames," to whom their primary instruction was entrusted.

The man first on this committee, and of course, the chairman, was Mr. Carter, and under their care were erected the little ten foot schoolhouses, one on the upper side of Winter street, where Master Vinal kept the North school, and the other on School street, where Master Sewall wielded the birch and taught the young idea how to shoot. The Jackman school traces its origin to the old schoolhouse which occupied essentially the same site, and the Kelly is the old North school – not on the original site but on land owned by Anthony Somerby, the first schoolmaster of old Newbury.

As a private citizen, he evidently believed in the future success of the town, as was shown by his large investment in land in various parts, not only of the new town, but also in parts of Newbury near its boundary. Even at an age of nearly four score years he was one of the foremost petitioners for the building of Essex Merrimac bridge, in which very useful but financially unprofitable ventures, he owned fifteen of the 200 shares.

Mr. Carter evidently believed in the successful development of the "North End," not only of Newburyport, but also of the old part of the town, and owned large tracts of land not only near the boundary line between the towns but between North street and Deer Island bridge.

In 1771, Mr. Carter bought from the estate of Archelaus Adams 4 acres, 156 rods of land for 118£ 10s ($395). This field measured 14 1-2 rods on High street, 55 rods of Broad street and 53 rods on Carter street, reaching to the bend in these streets. This "bend" comes from the fact that High street and Merrimac street are not parallel, hence the boundary between the lots laid out between these streets was not the same straight line. Mr. Carter also owned land between Carter and Buck streets. He died in 1798 and in division of his real estate this field passed into the possession of Mr. Smith of Boston. Had Mr. Carter lived a few years longer this tract of land would probably have been converted into house lots and the development of this part of the North End would have been more rapid.

The Carter field was for some reason kept in the Smith family until it was sold for division among heirs. Had the owner of this fine lot been willing to sell, it would undoubtedly have been developed some years earlier. It was said that "Signor"Papanti wished to buy it about 1850. Had he done so his fine house would have occupied a part of it.

The field was used as a pasture by Joseph Akerman while he had his slaughtering house near by where cattle and sheep, happily unconscious, awaited their doom.

On the level grounds Van Amburgh's menagerie once gave an exhibition, in a single tent without any circus accompaniment.

No part of this field was sold and no house was built on it until 1856.

Monroe street from Carter to Broad was laid out through this land in 1840, leaving a lot of 75 1-2 rods on Broad, Carter and the lower side of Monroe streets. This land was occupied by Mr. Papanti until his new house was built and after he vacated it, was sold at auction and four houses built on it; one on the corner of Broad and one on Monroe street by Richard Plumer; one on the corner of Monroe and Carter by Joseph Dockum and one on Carter street by Weston Clark.

The large field bounded by High, Broad, Monroe, and Carter streets, measuring 500 rods, was sold by the heirs of Smith to Richard Plumer and Alexander Brown in 1863 for $6000. Reserving for themselves two large lots on High street running down Broad to Carter the remainder of the field was offered for sale for house lots and the first lot of 50 rods on the corner of Broad and Monroe streets was bought by the writer in 1864 for $13 a rod.

There are no old houses on this tract of land but twelve modern houses varying somewhat in shape, style, size and cost, but all good, serviceable dwellings, ten of them being owned by the occupants. Two of these houses were costly, one being taxed on the assessors' books in 1878 for $11,000 and the other for $10,000, which was considered about two-thirds of their commercial value. The other houses ranged from $1000 to $3000.

The estate that easily stands first in beauty of location and in its surrounding is that of the late Alexander Brown. The large garden with great elm trees in front, the spacious house of pleasing style, the heavy, and solid wall that surrounds it, all mark this as one of the most elegant and valuable estates at the North End.

The estate next to Mr. Brown's on Broad street was laid out by Deacon Henry Payne in 1866 and '67. Upon a lot of land running from Broad to Carter, Mr. Payne built a large and expensive French roof cottage and stable, and laid out the grounds in an artistic manner with trees and shrubs.

Mr. Payne was a machinist and built the brick building below Market square afterwards occupied by John Stanley and more recently by Mr. Holker. Here Mr. Payne established his machine shop and expected to do much business but the disturbance in industrial affairs that followed the close of the civil war involved him, as it did many others, and his course was brief.

His house was a costly one, in fact all houses built at this time of depreciated currency were costly. The auctioneer who sold it stated that it cost $20,000; it sold, however, for about $8000. Capt. Joseph

Hoyt purchased the property and occupied it until his death when it passed into other hands and finally into the possession of Albert Sawyer. A few years after Mr. Sawyer bought it, the house caught fire and the upper story was destroyed. In rebuilding, the clumsy French roof was replaced by a story in colonial style with a tower, which gave to the house a much ore pleasing exterior.

The cottage next to the Sawyer house was built in 1807 or 1808 by John Dockum in 1866 *sic*; the next by Charles Lovejoy in 1897, the one on the corner of Broad and Monroe by O.B. Merrill in 1866. The house next below on Monroe street by Frank Downing in 1871, that on the corner of Carter and Monroe by O.W. Greaton in 1869, the store on Carter street by Philip Hennessey, the cottage next above by Greaton, the next house by Mr. Flanagan and the last house by Humphrey Haley, have all been built since 1870. [Following is a Merrill's correction given in Paper No. 7, to the above: "The cottage next below the Sawyer house was built by Mr. John F. Pearson in 1877 or 1878, and after some changes of ownership was brought by its present owner, Mr. Leroy Edwards. The house next below Mr. Edwards' was built in 1866 by John Dockum, and by his heirs sold to assistant Marshall John McLean in 1905. The Sawyer house was owned and occupied for a short time by Hon. Orrin J. Gurney. The house on the corner of Carter and Ocean streets was built about 1845 not 1858."]

The value of the Carter field in 1850 with no houses on it was about $7000; at present a conservative estimate of the same land with 16 dwelling houses would be between $50,000 and $60,000.

From the middle of Carter street to the southeast limit of the 20 acres that belonged to the homestead of Archelaus Adams was a strip of land 53 rods long and measuring about 3 and a half acres bought of the heirs of Adams by Green Morrill and others. The only old house built upon any part of this land was the large three story house now standing on the corner of Carter street and Cutter's court. In 1811 Abel Keyes bought a lot of land of 18.7 square rods, 115 feet long and 44 feet wide for $295, upon which he built and partly finished the house. This lot when bought was surrounded by private property and the deed stipulated that Mr. Keyes must find his own way out to a public road. Carter street had just been opened, nearly to his house, as well as the part of Monroe street, which joined it to Warren and Mr. Keyes evidently got out by acquiring the lot between his lot and Monroe street.

In 1840 this house became the property of Ellza Patten who sold it to James Frothingham, in 1845, from whom in 1850 it passed to Richard Fowler, by whom it was sold in 1867 to the Ocean mill.

No house was built on this part of the Adams land except the Keyes house until the building of the Ocean mill in 1845.

The first house built on the southeast side of Carter street was on the corner of Ocean and Carter by James Reed soon after 1858. It was owned and occupied for several years by the well known tonsorial artist, John Osborn, a gentleman of color. The group of houses on Warren and Ocean streets and Lafayette court were built by Horace Bickford. The house on the upper corner of Carter and Ocean streets was moved there from Washington street when the second railroad depot was built in 1853; this house with the next below and the six small cottages were owned by Mr. Papanti. The house on the corner of Eagle and Carter was built by Mr. Selfridge, and the one next below on Eagle street by the late John Akerman.

The house owned by Dr. Howe was built about 1853 by a carpenter named Pettingell and sold to Mr. Rogers of West Newbury from whom it passed to its present owner. The brick block which extends along Monroe street from Carter to Warren, was built by Albert Currier at the time when the Ocean mill was built by him, about 1845 or '46.

Summing up the Adams field of 20 acres, we find in it 70 dwelling houses, three-quarters of which are owned by the occupants and valued at about $150,000 or more than two percent, of all the real estate of the city. Truly this part of the North End at least has a value in its homes, having been almost entirely a residential district occupied by persons who, without being eminent for great wealth or highly exalted positions, have yet been people of good social standing, comparing favorable with other parts of the town in those mental and moral virtues that make up the character of good citizens."

O. B. MERRILL

NORTH END PAPERS. NO. 7

Newburyport Daily News, Saturday, July 7, 1906, p 8.

Archelaus Woodman, Archelaus Adams.

From 1618 to 1754.

People familiar with the history old Newbury know that the settlers in 1635 crowded together about the meeting house at Parker river, but that they soon tired of their small four acre lots and determined to improve some of their extensive domain. A map of the original lots is found on pg. 14 of Mr. Currier's "Old Newbury" and among the names of the settlers appears that of Archelaus Woodman. In 1644 "the lott layers" began to lay out the new town along the banks of the Merrimac river, extending from Artichoke river as far down as any habitations were likely to be, but reaching back from the river only as far as the lower street, which with shortened name became "Low" street, called the Lower street because it was on the low or meadow land, while the country road on the high land in distinction from the other was in the course of time called High street.

In the division of lots in the new town, Archelaus Woodman received a lot of 20 acres on Merrimac street. This was not the present street of that name along the river but the name was given by the town to the part of the present High street that runs by the head of Toppan street.

This was the 20 acres which the North End papers have sketched, which was directly opposite the 40 acres assigned to Edward Woodman which reached from the country road or Merrimack street down Toppan's lane, upon which Jacob Toppan's old house now stands. This division was probably in 1644 or a few years later. In subsequent divisions of the public land, Archelaus Woodman acquired much real estate, in various parts of the town, but as we are interested only in the 20 acres at the North End, his other land has not been considered. The first owner then of this land, as far as any definite record gives us exact knowledge was Archelaus Woodman.

The exact spot upon which Archelaus Woodman placed his house is not easily determined, but there is reason to believe that it was on Toppan's lane, on land owned by him or by his brother Edward. By the kindness of Isaac Little, Esq., who has given me a list of the "Tything men for 1695" –his residence can be approximately fixed.

In the Puritan system of civil government in which the church controlled the state, the tything man was a very important officer. It was his duty "to have inspection and look over families that they attend the publick worship of God and do not break the Sabbath." In 1695 Newbury had twenty tything men, each having charge of about 10 families. Tything district number sixteen extended from Woodmans' lane, now Kent street, about as far as the Plains. The tything man for this district was Moses Pilsbury and he had charge of the families of Lieut. Woodman, Lieut. Toppan, Mr. John Sewall, Mr. Pilsbury, Samuel and Joseph Poore and the Widow Davis.

Lieut. Woodman was Archelaus; Lieut. Toppan was Jacob, who built the old house now standing; John Sewall was "Mr." if not lieut. These three men lived on or near Toppan's lane. Sam and Joseph Poore probably lived near the river and the Pilsbury's between Toppan's lane and the Plains. A map of the West parish made in 1729 and found in Mr. Currier's Old Newbury, page 392, gives a house on the Curson's mill road occupied by Archelaus Woodman. This man was the son of Edward, and the nephew of the older Archelaus Woodman. In 1706 the older Archelaus Adams gave Sam Sewall two acres with dwelling house and orchard on the southeast side of Toppan's land, in exchange for two acres of land and 30£ in money. This may have been the house in which his grandfather Woodman had lived, but the registry of deeds does not warrant the certainty of it.

Having located this old Puritan pioneer as well as we can, the question of interest arises, who he was and whence he came. "Archelaus Woodman," says Dr. Savage in his genealogical dictionary, "named Hercules in the report to the government of passengers from Southampton in the James of London, -- embarked April 6th and arrived here June 3, 1635 called Mercer of Malford." "Perhaps the custom house officers know more of Hercules than of the other name, though both are equally heathenish, but probably the sound was not unlike." "He was born in 1618, but how entitled Mercer when only a minor, provoked enquiry." "My conjecture is that his elder brother Edward deserves that description and came in that ship, but it was undesirable to give his name and excite suspicion that he was not authorized under the odious orders of the country to come to our country."

The meaning of Dr. Savage evidently was, that the boy Archelaus was made to personate his brother Edward, who being a man of strong character and a stubborn Puritan, was well known to the authorities. Both the elder and the younger were skilful enough, however, to hoodwink the dull servants of the king who by the Grace of God was sovereign of Great Britain, Ireland and France.

The name of young Woodman seemed to puzzle the custom house officers and with reason, for it was a name entirely foreign to their time, but belonged away back to old Grecian times. How any good Puritan came to give this name to a child is a mystery, although the word is very smooth in sound when pronounced in four syllables as it should be. Its meaning in the Greek is leader of the people—a title that would have well applied to his brother, Edward. Probably the name was a family name, given by a scholarly ancestor familiar with the writings of the old Greeks. In deeds of land in which young Woodman was afterwards concerned, he is called Hercules as often as Archelaus. He was registered by the custom house officer as mercer—that is merchant, but being a minor had no legal title to anything higher than apprentice. Difficulties were placed in the way of those who wished to leave the old country, and the Puritan colony, although more of a business venture than a religious one, and made up of men of influence was jealously watched by the servants of King Charles, who wished his subjects to remain at home and do as they were told by the religious rulers.

We find on the records very little about Archelaus Woodman. His name appears occasionally in performance of civic duties, and also as lieutenant of the militia and he was simply a good Puritan of no remarkable prominence. That he was a shrewd and careful business man is evident from the fact that he accumulated a considerable fortune in real estate not only in Newbury, but in other towns.

As the end of the century approached and Mr. Woodman was bearing heavily the weight of four score years naturally he desired to be free from the care of his large estate, and as he wished that his real estate should be kept together rather than divided, he executed a deed in 1698, by which his property was practically entailed according to the old English custom. This deed covers four large closely written pages of volume fourteen in Essex Registry of Deeds, in the parchment covered book where it was copied more than two hundred years ago.

Mr. Woodman left no son, and by this deed his property was conveyed to his grandson Archelaus Adams. It conveys "my now dwelling house, barn and out houses * * * with all the tillage land, pasture, marsh, and meadow, free hold lots, and rate lots, wood, timber, fences, trees, springs, orchards, gardens, yards, wells, water courses, with all estates, rights, and interests of demand."

The conditions were, that the old gentleman and his wife be cared for during the remainder of their lives, that they be paid by Adams' 40£ a year; that they have a certain number of cows and sheep, for whom "barne" room should be provided, and finally that the old people be provided with a definite about of firewood and other things needed for their comfort. Certain penalties or forfeits were provided in case the conditions were not carried out. In this way Mr. Woodman's real estate came into the possession of Archelaus Adams.

We find upon the town records nothing about Mr. Adams, but he seemed to have kept together property received from his grandfather until his death some time after 1750. His will on file at Salem is dated 1753, by which and by a deed, he evidently meant to entail the property to his son John in the way in which it had come to him form Archelaus Woodman. This disposition of the property was not pleasing to the other heirs and an attempt was made to break the entail.

In volume 100, page 230 of Essex Registry of Deeds, we find that Joseph Dow of Salisbury sues John Adams, claiming that Adams had "without judgment and unjustly debarred him from the use of certain land laid out to the right of Archelaus Woodman deceased; that the said John Brown is seized of the lands aforesaid and for barring out all estate entail, etc." In Volume 180, page 190 A; we find as follows: "At his majesty's inferior court of common pleas, Joseph Dow of Salisbury against John Adams of Newbury demands of John the several tracts of land hereinafter mentioned." "Dow claims that he has been unjustly disseized by Hugh Hunt within 30 years of certain parts of this property, and that he is still kept out of it by Adams." "That a tenant, Edward Hubbard, was enjoying the value of 10£ a year." "Afterwards Dow came into court in person and Hubbard through somemnly called, came not again but departed in contempt of court and made default." This records does not of course give all the particulars of the trial, but the result was to break the entail, and in

1754 John Adams "gave up his entail" of lands from Woodman upon the payment from the other heirs of the nominal sum of 1£ – 17 s 4 (6.23.)

In volume 100 of Essex deeds spoken of above is given a list f the various pieces of real estate as Adams received them from Woodman. One item in this list and the only one that has to do with our subject, is the "twenty acres between Woodman's Lane and Moody's Lane," joining Woodman's land on one side, and Moody's on the other. The breaking of the entail brought this land into the market for sale, as has already been described in the North End papers.

Addenda –In North End papers No. 5, the date of the death of Edward Bass should have been 1858 instead of 1851. In paper No. 6, the sentence following the sketch of the Sawyer's house should read—the cottage next below the Sawyer house was built by Mr. John F. Pearson in 1877 or 1878, and after some changes of ownership was bought by its present owner, Mr. Leroy Edwards. The house next below Mr. Edmands' was built in 1866 by John Dockum, and by his heirs sold to assistant Marshal John McLean in 1905. The Sawyer house was owned and occupied for a short time by Hon. Orrin J. Gurney. The house on the corner of Carter and Ocean streets was built about 1845 not 1858. The North End paper of June 30th was No. 6 and the subject was Carter's Field.

O. B. MERRILL.

NORTH END PAPERS. NO. 8

Newburyport Daily News, Saturday, July 14, 1906, p 7.

North, Tyng, Broad and Carter Streets.
From 1796 to 1848.

In 1714-15 Merrimac street was laid out two rods wide from Market street to Woodman's lane. It is probable that as early as 1750 the desirable building lots, first on the lower or river side and then on the upper side had been taken up. At this time John and Richard Kent, who owned nearly all the land from Woodman's lane to North street, opened the road two rods wide. In 1772 John Kent sold to Tracy land "on a two rod way laid out by John and Richard Kent from Woodman's lane to Moody's land and the lane there; "that is from Woodman's lane to Woodland street. In 1758 the town of Newbury voted "to receive and repair the way to be laid out by Deacon John and Richard Kent and Moses Moody."

Lots were sold and houses built on the river side of this road, and when the best sites had been sold. Warren street was opened in 1780, Kent street in 1788 and Dove street about 1795. The development on these streets was healthy, the lots sold being for the building of houses.

The opening of Broad, Tyng and North streets came after the best lots near Merrimac street, had been sold and seems to have resulted from an attempt to open a more desirable class of building lots on the high land. With this movement was a great deal of speculation – a large part of the land towards High street being sold not for building purposes but for a "rise." The "boom" started with Broad, weakened with Tyng and "flatted out" entirely with North street. Much money was sunk by the wily promoters as well as by their victims.

The design of opening Broad, Tyng and North streets was evidently framed at the same time.

The first evidence that we have by a deed as to the opening of any one of them, is the conveyance to Thomas Emery in 1796 of the lot on the upper corner of North and High streets, in which provision is made by Moody on the upper side and Tyng on the lower side to open a street four rods wide. It is probable that this lane was opened long before this time as a means of approach to an old Pilsbury house on Merrimac street, and to the landing at the river.

The formation of the land through which this lane ran was such as to make an easy road for horses and oxen, while the land through which Tyng and Broad were opened was hilly and unsafe. No lane by which the waterside could be approached between Woodman's and Moody's lanes is mentioned in any deed on record.

The land through which these three streets passed was owned in colonial days by Richard Kent, Sr., the part through which North and Tyng passed was owned in 1797 by a speculator or promoter of his time named Major David Coffin. In the warrant for the town meeting of March, 1801, is an article: "To see if the town will accept a street laid out by the selectman, called North street, agreeable in the petition of D.A. Tyng and Major David Coffin."

The part of North street laid out by Moody was probably the half on the Newbury side for the whole length of the street; on the lower side Tyng owned the upper part and David Coffin the lower towards Merrimac street. At the town meeting of March 17th, 1801, it was voted that "Stephen Cross, Benj. Balch and Timothy Palmer be a committee to examine the situation of North street and report at the adjourned meeting." At the adjourned meeting in May no report was made nor at any subsequent meeting. Timothy Palmer was at the time surveyor of highways, and competent to judge of the need of a new street here. Very likely the fact that the upper side was in Newbury, and that the old town was unwilling to improve its part, may have determined the matter. A careful search of the town records fails to find any action in regard to this street or Tyng street until many years after both were opened.

The date of the opening of Tyng street has been a matter of conjecture. It was taken for granted that it was opened in 1805, but an examination of deeds on record at Salem, shows that the street was opened in 1797. As has been stated in a previous North End paper, Thomas Thomas bought the land from Broad street to the middle of Tyng in the spring of 1797. Wishing to realize on his purchase as soon as possible, he, with Thos. Coker, who owned the land on the upper side, and Major Coffin, who owned the land between their land and Merrimac street laid out Tyng street. The proof of this is found in a deed given in May 1797, not more than a month or two after Thomas bought the land of Charles Jackson, in which Thomas sells to

Stephen Toppan 51 rods of land for $512 "on a new street laid out by myself and Coker from High to Merrimac." This land was the lot upon which Humphrey Webster built the three story house near the head of the street.

This fact is to be emphasized as it fixes the date of the opening of this street. The only streets described on the town book are Kent and Broad. One object that I have had in mind in the North End papers and upon which I have expended much care and research, has been to fix the date when the streets above Kent street were opened. I take for granted that when a deed of land is given upon a way opened or laid down, that then the road, to all intents and purposes as far as the building of houses and establishment of homes is concerned, is opened. The acceptance of a way by a town is no evidence at all of its place in the development of a neighborhood. In 1834 Warren street was accepted by the town, it was laid out about 1780; house lots began to be sold there in 1782 and in the year 1800 a dozen houses stood upon the street.

It may then be accepted as a fact to be proved by the registry of deeds that Tyng street was opened in 1797. There is no evidence that it was ever accepted by the town, but that is of little consequence the street is there, has been there and is likely to be there in the future.

An interesting subject in regard to this street is its name. It was first called the "New street," then the "first new street above Broad," "a new street some times called North;" a mortgage deed given of the hospital property called it "Goodwin's lane," another mortgage deed calls it "Walnut" street; another deed probably made by an admirer of the great Democrat calls it "Jefferson street." A small pamphlet that belonged to my grandfather, Jos. Babson, Jr. entitled the "Rules of Dernier Resorte" – a volunteer fire association formed in 1761, and which contained a list of the members with the residence of each – has "Joseph Babson, Jr., Tyng street." This pamphlet was printed in 1816, and proved that the name "Tyng" was applied to the street at that time. On page 346 of Mr. Currier's History of Newburyport, this fact is mentioned. After Mr. Currier's book was printed, however, I found upon the assessor's book for the year 1809, a lot of land on "Tyng street," taxed to Wm. Bartlett, but the same lot sold a few years previous by Thomas Coker to Moses Hale is located "on a street opened by me." It is plain that the street got its name from Dudley A. Tyng who owned the large three story house directly opposite the head of the street from 1799 to 1804. It was the wealth and prominence of Tyng rather than his ownership of land that gave the name to the street. Not until about 1830 were the old names discarded and the street called by its present name.

The first mention of Broad street in town records is found in the selectmen's book for 1794. In the warrant for the March meeting of that year article 12 is "to see if the town will accept a four rod way laid down by Nathaniel Carter and others, by the name of Broad street." In the town meeting of March 13th, 1794, it was voted to postpone acting on Article 12, respecting laying out Broad street, till adjournment." The report of the adjourned meeting makes no mention of any action upon article 12, and for some reason the matter was for the time dropped.

In June 1794, the legislature had ordered a careful survey to be made of each town in the state, and Sept. 18, 1794, the town voted that "the selectmen take, or cause to be taken, an accurate plan of the town and lodge the same in the secretary's office." The town fathers not being themselves sufficiently expert with chain and compass employed Joseph Somerby to take or make a survey of the town according to law. Mr. Somerby was a careful and accurate surveyor and several plans made by him are found in the first and second volume of the town records.

Mr. Somerby made his map and in 1795 deposited it in the office of the secretary of state, where Mr. Currier found it and had it copied for his history of Newburyport, where it may be found on page 22 of that interesting volume. Mr. Somerby was the surveyor who laid out Broad street. It is probable that the plan of opening this street as well as Tyng and North was formed as early as 1790, and that Broad street was fenced out about 1793. After 1794 nothing appears on the town record in regard to Broad street until 1796 when the warrant for the annual town meeting in March, called upon the voters for, their sanction for opening Harris, Pleasant, Essex, Broad and Birch streets. The town meeting of March 17th, 1796, approved the opening of all these streets except Essex and Broad. The consideration of these two streets was referred to the adjourned meeting of April 4th which approved the laying out and acceptance of both these streets.

We do not know why opposition was made to opening Broad street, but probably some owner of land demanded damages. The street was laid out through the land of the heirs of Patrick Tracy on the northwest side, and of Nathaniel Carter on the southeast side, a distance of 867 feet to the "bend," hence through land of Mariner

Kent on the northwest side, and of Joshua and Abel Kent with Samuel Pillsbury on the southeast, 693 feet to Merrimac, making the entire length 1560 feet.

On page 135 of the second volume of town records is found a plan of the street made by Eben March from the survey by Somerby. The description reads thus: Beginning on Merrimac street four feet above the dwelling house of Samuel Pilsbury, 3rd, running south 61 degrees, 15 minutes west, 10 chains and 50 length; thence south 57 degrees west, 13 chains, 15 links to High street, with a width of four rods." Signed by Theop. L. Bradbury, John Pettingill, Daniel Horton and Eben Stickney, Selectmen.

One very desirable feature in the opening of this street was that it was made four rods wide or 66 feet wide, and this seemed to fix the width also of Tyng and North streets. Warren street had been made only 40 feet wide and Dove only 30, while Carter street opened in 1811 was only made three rods or about 50 feet wide. In 1790 no street above Market was four rods wide and many streets soon lined with houses deserve the title of alleys rather than of streets. The men who laid out Green street in 1782 thought they were doing a very generous act in making it four rods wide. The lanes laid out in the early days were in general only two rods wide. Merrimac street which the land owners must have known would be one of the streets in continual use, was laid out in this way, entailing much cost upon future generations in widening it. High street by some lucky chance escaped this narrowing process probably because it was laid out upon the common land.

Carter street in 1811 had been opened only to Monroe, in 1848 it was continued to Merrimac street through land of Deacon John Pearson which formerly belong to Joshua Kent. Mr. Pearson spent much time and thought in laying out this street, and made so many calculations that as suggestion was made that it be named "Calculation street." These four streets then reaching from High to Merrimac were opened through the land that was granted to Archelaus Woodman and to Richard Kent, Sr., when the new town was opened along the Merrimac.

O. B. MERRILL

NORTH END PAPERS. NO. 9

Newburyport Daily News, Saturday, July 21, 1906, p 5.

Deacon John Kent and His Land.
From 1747 to 1812.

Deacon John Kent was an officer in the church of the Third Parish in Newbury, now the Pleasant street church. He was elected deacon in 1747-48. As this kind of double date occurs often in affairs previous to 1752, it may need explanation.

There were in old times two ways of naming the beginning of the year. The so called "old style" began the year in March; the "new style" in January. By the old style January, February, and a part of March belonged to the same years as the previous December.

In the date given above, if Mr. Kent's election took place in January, it would be in 1747, according to the old style, but in 1748 by the new style.

The Puritan began the year on March 25th, and rejected not only the new style, but also the names of the months, as heathenish, and instead of calling the months by their present names, he called them by number. This custom, however, seemed to apply to spiritual rather than to temporal affairs. When his real estate was concerned he paid tribute to mammon as well as to righteousness by giving the double date – the penultimate figure for the old style, and the final figure for the new style.

In 1752 the English parliament passed an act adopting the "new style;" the old style was dropped both in England and America, and the year began in January, in spite of the heathenish origin of the name of that month.

The land on the upper side of Merrimac street from Woodman's Lane to North street belonged to Richard and Deacon John Kent. Deacon John made his will in 1778 – he gives "it to his son Abel the house he, Abel, lived in, and the river lot by the town landing."

This was probably the house now standing next to Creeden's store on the lower side of Kent street. It stood then down about to the present railroad track and was moved to its present location when the street was widened. In 1795 Abel Kent sold this house to Jona. Mason, who the same year sold it to Captain Orne, with 46 rods of land for £275 ($917). To his son John the deacon left one-third of the land southeast of the house he then lived in. His house was the one now standing on the upper corner of Dove and Merrimac. To his son Joshua, "one-third of the lot adjoining his house with the land northwest of John's house;" Joshua's house was the one now occupied by Miss Ann Sanderson who is a lineal descendent of Joshua.

At the death of Joshua, this house was purchased by the late Deacon John Pearson.

To his son Stephen, Deacon John left land adjoining Joshua's on the northwest, and to his son Benjamin three acres on the southwest side of Merrimac street between land of his brother Richard. To his daughters Abigail Pettingill, Mary Pilsbury, and Rebecca Burroughs he left 13£, 9 s, 8 d. ($44.93) to each, with all his household goods. His real estate not disposed of by will was to be divided among the five sons.

A tradition exists that the good deacon with true fatherly affection gave each of his sons a house upon his marriage. If this is true, it fixes the date of the building of the houses mentioned above as early as 1778, if not earlier. It is hardly to be believed that the deacon, while providing shelter for his sons, left his daughters out in the cold. If he was this generous with Rebecca, Abigail and Mary, his action gives a clue to the building of several houses about whose origin the registry of deeds has nothing.

In 1788 the heirs of Deacon John and Richard gave the land for opening Kent street, and in 1779, John Kent sold to George Burroughs two and a half acres of land inherited from his father, bounded northeast by Merrimac street; southeast by Thos. Merrill and Richard Kent, southwest by heirs of Jacob Sawyer, and northwest by Joshua Kent. The price paid for the land with the house on the corner of Dove street was £2100, ($7000). The deed does not state the price of money paid, but it was probably paper money worth much less than 100 cents to the dollar.

Through this land Burroughs opened a way 40 feet wide. The name "Warren" afterwards given it, may be accounted for by the fact that several soldiers of the revolution lived on this street. In 1796 Mariner Kent sold the land for a street two rods wide afterwards named Dove street. Tradition says that a small schooner was built in the backyard of one of the houses, and moved on rollers to the river, and that the name of the craft was "The Dove."

The house in which Rebecca Burroughs lived was the large gambrel roof house directly opposite the foot of Dove street. The size, style of finish and general aspect of this dwelling shows that it was a first class house for the time of its erection.

In 1762 John Kent sold to Thomas Burroughs the lot upon which the house stands, on the northeast side of "a two rod way." In 1794 and 1796 John Hoyt, and Thomas Burroughs, gentleman, quit claim to David Hoyt their interest in this estate. From the heirs of Hoyt it passed into possession of Henry Merrill and from him to its present owner. The land on the corner of Broad and Merrimac passed into possession of some members of the Pillsbury family several years before the opening of Broad street, but no deed is on records which gives the date. The oldest deed on record is in 1800, when Sam Pillsbury, 3rd, sold the house and 32 rods of land to Capt. Hovey, and Hovey to Henry Merrill, Sr., who conveyed it to his son, Henry, Jr., by whom it was occupied many years.

Sam Pilsbury's deed to Hovey says that he received it from his father. It is probable that in some unrecorded way some one of Dea. John's daughters was concerned in the ownership of this house.

Another estate equally puzzling is the house on Broad street nearest the pump. In 1796 this was owned by Capt. John Hoyt, but no deed on record shows when it came into his possession. Hoyt's wife, however, was the daughter of Rebecca Burroughs, and in 1799, Rebecca, widow of Thomas Buroughs, quit claims to John Hoyt the land and buildings, thus showing that one of the daughters of Dea. John was concerned in the ownership of this house.

In 1840 the heirs of Hoyt sold the property to Alfred Pilsbury and in 1841 Pilsbury sold it to William Choate, ship joiner, for $650.

Another old house with which Dea. John's daughter Mary was concerned was the old house opposite the foot of North street, torn down when the factory building now there, was built. In 1773 Sam Pilsbury, husband of Mary Kent, bought of John and Richard Kent two and a half acres of land with a well for £50 ($167), bounded southwest by Merrimac street and northeast by the river. The Pilsbury family record speaks of this old house as through built by Pilsbury. The statement may be questioned. The old house, low studded and with the roof sloping nearly to the ground in the rear, with small windows and ancient finish, belonged to a style of dwellings in use many years before the time of Pilsbury. Pilsbury was a boat builder and had his shop on land in the rear of the old house.

A successful boat builder must be an ingenious mechanic, and he certainly would not have built a new house after a style of the preceding century.

It is possible that the two acres and a half did not include the old house, but was the lot below upon which the gambrel roof house was afterwards built. The old house may have been acquired by Pilsbury later. The northwest bound of this lot when bought by Pilsbury was land of Richard Kent, and very likely this old house had been owned by some earlier generation of the Kent family. The genealogical record referred to, also gives the wife of Sam Pilsbury as the daughter of Abel Kent, when in fact she was the sister of Abel.

In 1796 the land through which North, Tyng and Broad streets were opened was owned by Mariner Kent; son of Richard Kent. In 1789 Mariner Kent bought of Benj. Kent two acres, 149 rods of land on Merrimac street bounded on the southwest by land of Coker and Tracy for £57 ($150); the same year he bought of Richard Kent 3 acres for £60 ($200), and soon after 3 acres more of Richard Kent for £60. This tract of land extended from the middle of North to Broad street. In 1797 Mariner Kent sold to Major David Coffin 8 1-4 acres, measuring 35 1-3 rods on Merrimac street; 34 1-2 on the northwest, by land of Moody and Carter; 34 1-3 rods on the southwest by land of Coker, Tyng and Thomas, and 38 1-2 on Broad street. All this land with the buildings for $1500.

Coffin was a speculator and promoter and bought this land for speculative purposes. He at once began to sell house lots. At first several lots on Merrimac street and a few on North were sold by Coffin at from $15, down to $8 or $10 a rod, but in a few years the demand for lots at these prices ceased.

Coffin kept the unsold land until 1812 when he managed to "unload" it upon two wealthy merchants of the town. In 1812 he mortgaged to Moses Brown the land between Broad and Tyng, 473 rods, with some other property for $12,000, and to Luther Waterman two-thirds of 280 rods on North street, with 340 rods on Merrimac street for $5500, probably getting about 10 times what it cost him in 1797.

The question naturally arises how such shrewd business men as Brown and Waterman could be thus "worked" by such a well known speculator. The answer is plain. Both men had acquired large fortunes in the balmy days of the town; in spite of the war, the embargo and the bad effects of the rule of the party that ruined the old Federalists, they believed that the good times must return. Alas, for their hopes – the old town at the close of the war with England went into a Rip Van Winkle sleep from which it did not wake for 25 years. Brown and Waterman died and left these mortgages to their heirs. Not a rod of this land from Broad to North was sold until 1843, and then only at a price such as did not pay the interest, much less the principle, of the original mortgage.

O. B. MERRILL

NORTH END PAPERS. NO. 10

Newburyport Daily News, Saturday, July 28, 1906, p 7.

Houses on Kent Field North to Carter Street.

From 1796 to 1848.

    The large tract of land between Tyng street and North, mortgaged by Coffin to Brown and Waterman was not redeemed by him, -- in fact, he soon afterwards made a deed giving up his equity in the premises. Only two houses were built upon the land before 1843, namely one at the foot of North, and the large three story double house on Tyng street. In 1800 David Coffin sold to Timothy Osgood 36 rods of land for $375, about $16 a rod, "on Merrimac street to a new street to be laid down." Coffin and Tyng petitioned the town the year following to "lay down" the street, but without success. The street was opened without doubt in 1800, but had not been accepted by the town. Osgood built his house there soon after 1800, as the assessors' book for 1800 shows him taxed for house and land $600, assessed value, which represented a commercial value of not less than $1200. In 1811 Coffin sold Osgood a small lot above his house on North street for $72. In 1815 Timothy sold to Samuel Osgood the house and 40 1-2 rods of land for $2000. In 1824 Samuel conveyed the property back to the heirs of Timothy, and in 1837 Isaac, one of the heirs, sold it to John Pearson, who in 1837 conveyed it to True Choate for $700 from whose heirs it passed to Mr. Cheney, the present owner.

    The other house upon the Waterman lot was the three story house on the northwest side of Tyng street, which was probably built by Mariner Kent between 1788 and 1797 as it was there when Coffin bought the land of Kent in 1797. This solid and substantial house is just as it was built except perhaps for the ell in the rear.

    The fields between Tyng and Broad mortgaged to Moses Brown in 1812, had on it three houses only, until 1843. The large double house of three stories on Merrimac street is the first which, except for the ells, is a perfect pattern of the one on Tyng street. In 1799, Benjamin Choate bought of David Coffin a lot 45 feet on the street; at the same time John Buzzell bought of Coffin a lot of 45 feet, adjoining Choate's lot, and upon the combined lots they built the house at once. On the assessors' book for 1800, the house is taxed for $1200. In 1827, Choate bought Buzzell's part and the house was owned by the heirs of Choate until a comparatively recent time. The next three story house was built by Moses and Nathan Coffin, probably soon after 1800. In 1809 it was sold to Oliver Spalding for $1000; in 1812 Spalding sold it to Timothy Dow, and Dow in 1816 sold it to Wm. Freeman for $1500, and he in 1818 conveyed it to Elkanah Freeman, who sold it to Converse Francis in 1819 for $600, from whom it passed in 1822 to Wm. Mace for $690, and finally to Ezekiel Choate who occupied it for many years until he built his new house on the upper corner of Merrimac and Oakland streets.

The third house was on Broad street now owned and occupied by Mr. Kimball; it was built and partly finished by Nathan Coffin about 1811. In 1812 it was sold to Capt. Joseph Buntin, and in 1824, Thomas Buntin sold it to Amos Wood. In 1826 Wood bought the large lot above the house upon which a new house stands. Mr. Wood was in his time quite a politician, of the old Whig party. He represented the town in the House of Representatives in 1852, '53 and '54.

In 1875, the heirs of Mr. Wood sole the estate to Wm. H. Huse and he to Obed W. Greaton the same year. Mr. Greaton built the new house above in Mr. Wood's orchard and afterwards exchange the old house with James Hart, tailor, for the cottage where he now lives on North Atkinson street.

The first lots sold for building purposes were on the lower side of Broad street. In 1796 Benj. Cross, cordwainer in lawyer's language, shoemaker, in common parlance, bought of Joshua Kent, 22 rods of land for $105 and built thereon the house now owned by Hiram Leach. In 1803 Mr. Cross sold the house and land to Parker Roberts for $950. In 1811 Roberts bought of Joshua Kent a strip of land below the house two rods on the streets and measuring 17 square rods for $308, about $18 a rod, a very considerable rise in value from the price paid in 1796 – of less than $5 a rod. Parker Roberts had two sons who were prominent half a century ago. One was the well known grocer, Parker Roberts, who for many years had a grocery store on the corner of State and Liberty streets. The other son was Joseph Roberts, the first alderman elected by ward six in 1851. Mr. Roberts was a watchmaker and jeweler and his place of business was in an old building on the corner of Merrimac street and Coleman's wharf. Mr. Roberts was a man of good ability, of strict integrity, and equal character and influence to his associates upon the new city government. Mr. Roberts was re-elected in 1852 and in August of that year he died.

Here it may be said that since the time of Mr. Roberts, ten residents of Broad street have served in the city government, giving eight years of service in the aldermanic branch and 15 years in the council. The board of school committee and overseers of the poor have also been represented by residents upon this street. In 1866, the heirs of Roberts sold the property to Hiram Leach whose skill and ingenuity converted the old house into a convenient and beautiful modern residence.

The house now owned by Moses Coffin was built by Mr. Wead, "cordwainer," who in 1796 bought of Abel Kent, then living in Maine, 51 rods of land for $247. Mr. Wead made and sold shoes at his store in Market square. Like most master mechanics he had apprentices and apprentices had a bad habit of running away. The old newspapers abound in advertisements of such runaways. Rewards were offered from half a cent, to several dollars depending somewhat upon the value of the absconder's labor. One of Mr. Wead's incipient cordwainers had the temerity to desert his lap stone and depart.

In July, 1803, an advertisement by Mr. Wead appears in the Herald. "Ran away. An indented apprentice Nathan Daggett, 5 feet 3 inches, in height." "Had on blue nankeen jacket and brown trousers. Masters of vessels and others are warned against harboring him,"-- A reward of ten dollars was offered for returning him, which shows that his services were valuable. Had he returned to his master his reward would have been a liberal dose of "strap oil" an old fashioned but valuable remedy for youthful faults, to be had only from a shoemaker.

In 1800 Mr. Wead sold the house and 35 rods of land to Jeremiah Sawyer for $1500.

The same year Sawyer advertised the house for sale "with a well near by," and in the same advertisement offers for sale two chaises. Sawyer was a chaise maker and had a shop in Belleville. Mead's deed to Sawyer conveys a quarter part of this well; Cross' deed to Roberts another quarter, the third quarter being owned by Capt. Hoyt and the fourth quarter by Moses Collin.

Before the introduction of the city water this old well did excellent service, its supply of pure and wholesome water never failing.

Sawyer mortgaged this property to Thos. Coker, and Coker sold it to Thos. Clark, who in 1801, sold it to John Carr for $1200. In this house was born Deacon John Carr of the old firm of Carr, Brown and Co., comb makers.

Deacon Carr was for many years an officer of the Whitefield church, a man of sterling integrity and a successful business man, loved and respected by all who knew him.

In 1822, Mr. Carr bought of Dr. Chas. Coffin 32 rods of land above his house and in 1823, 31 rods adjoining this from Nathaniel Dodge. His whole estate cost Mr. Carr not less than $300. After the death of Mr. Carr and his wife, the whole estate was told to Emery Coffin in 1831 for $600.

The house next that of Sam. Pillsbury, 3rd, was built by Benjamin Pilsbury, who in 1803 bought 23 rods of land for $200, and in 1810 bought another lot adjoining. The house was probably built soon after 1803. After Pilsbury's death it passed to Winthrop O. Evans, an ingenious ship joiner, one of the class of skilful mechanics trained by Benj. Choate. Mr. Evans sold the house to the late John M. Carter, and he to Mrs. Downes, who converted it into a double tenement.

The three story house next above was built by John Pilsbury about 1814. In that year he bought of Sam. Pilsbury 22 rods with a small building for $400. In 1845 we find it advertised for sale by the heirs of John Pilsbury, when it passed into possession of W. O. Evans.

This house was probably the last built on any part of the land between Warren street and North until 1843.

This paper concludes the sketch of the houses on North, Tyng and Broad streets that were built near the end of the eighteenth, or in the early part of the nineteenth century.

These houses were built to last, of excellent material and by faithful workman and are good for as many years of service in the future as they have been in the past.

In 1843 the value of the land between North and Tyng street – about 550 rods with two houses was not far from $1800. In 1843, the part of this land owned by the heirs of Waterman was sold, and houses began to be built on North and Tyng streets. There are now on this block of land 16 houses worth approximately $25,000. The lot of 473 rods owned in 1843 by the heirs of Moses Brown, together with three houses and land, was valued in 1843 about $2800; in 1905, 23 houses and other building on this block of land between Tyng and Broad streets were worth not less than $40,000.

Thus it will be seen that the eight and a quarter acres sold by Mariner Kent to David Coffin in 1797 for $1500, had increased in value in 1843 to about $4600, but between 1843 and 1905 it had made an addition to its value of about 900 per cent. The building of houses from 1843 indicates a slow but healthy growth, true not only of the region described but of a larger territory adjoining.

Carter street from Merrimac street to Cutter's court, was opened in 1848, through the Kent land, then owned by Dea. John Pearson. Having been opened less that 60 years, it has no old houses upon its borders. Stephen Pike and Samuel Cheney each built a house for his own use, but nearly all the other houses erected were tenements, for use principally of operatives in the Ocean mill.

Albert Currier built for this purpose six two story cottages soon after the street was opened and a few years later Thomas Atwood built three story and a half cottages on the lower side of the street. At present nearly all these tenement houses have come into possession of people who occupy them. There are now on the street 23 houses with an approximate value of about $15,000.

O. B. MERRILL

NORTH END PAPERS. NO. 11

Newburyport Daily News, Saturday, August 4, 1906, p 7.

Houses on Warren, Kent and Dove Streets.

North End paper No. 10 gave a sketch of the old houses as far as Carter street on Merrimac. This paper continues the account of houses on the upper side of Merrimac to Kent and then of those on the river side of that street from Kent to North street.

The house on the corner of Carter and Merrimac, owned once and occupied by Miss Sanderson was built by Dea. John Kent for his son, Joshua, as early as 1778 and probably some earlier. Joshua in 1778 was 38 years old and was probably married before that time, and if his marriage brought him a house as well as a wife this house must be nearly 150 years of age.

Mr. Kent was an organ builder and his shop was a small building below his house on Merrimac Street. Some years after Mr. Kent's death when the premises were owned by Dea. Pearson, an ancient schoolmarm "kept school" there. Several long seats without backs served to accommodate a score or more of squirming youngsters who studied the pictures in Emerson's primary arithmetic, or puzzled out the words in a spelling book, while "Aunt Hannah" worked away on a blue stocking with her knitting needles. A boy who was troublesome did penance standing in a flour barrel.

The house on the upper corner of Merrimac and Warren was the home of Samuel Coffin, father of Capt. Abel, who after his return from service in the continental army built the house in which he passed the remainder of his life. Mr. Coffin with several of the men who lived at the "North End" enlisted in Capt. Newell's company that marched to Bunker Hill in April 1775. The land upon which this house was built was bought of George Burroughs in 1787, and the house erected soon after.

Mr. Coffin was a soldier of the Revolution who fought at Bunker Hill, at Germantown and in other engagements. In the same company with Coffin was John Brett whose home was on Warren street.

On the lower corner of Warren there stood 70 years ago an old house and barn owned in the early part of the century by Samuel Emerson. In 1837 James Blood bought the property through Nathaniel Boardman for $450. The old buildings were removed and Mr. Blood built for his own residence a mansion that for elegance and cost was far in advance of any residence of the times. A few years after its erection it barely escaped destruction by the burning of a barn in the rear of Sargent's house directly opposite. This fire broke out on a fearfully cold night in winter, and the firemen who worked the old hand tubs were covered with ice. Mr. Blood lavished much care and labor upon this house and especially upon his garden. The "Blood grape" came from his garden from a raisin seed planted by him.

Warren street was opened about 1780 and soon after house lots began to be sold. In 1782, Jas. Merrill bought 60 rods on the lower side for 150£ ($500). And the same year Nath. Torrey bought 10 rods for 30£, ($100). In 1785 R. Stockman, block maker, bought 12 rods on the upper side of the new street for 25£, 4s, ($84). In 1782 John Brett, cabinet maker, bought 18 rods on the upper side, and in 1787, Jos. Whiting, bricklayer, bought 30 rods on the upper side.

These lots were bought, not for speculation, but for the building of houses, as is evident from the assessors' book for 1800 on which we find houses taxed to Michael Norton $400; to Jonathan Stickney, $400; to Joseph Whiting, $800; to Jonathan Merrill, $500; to Dan Merrill, $400; to Wm. Middleton, $600; to John Brett, house and shop, $800; to James Chase, $700 and $400; to Wm. Creasey, $400. These figures are assessor's valuation; the real worth of these houses was from $800 to $1200. It is probably that nearly all these houses are now standing upon Warren street, many of them built over and modernized.

There are very few new houses on the old part of Warren street which extended only to Monroe street. Soon after 1845, Mr. Blood built a block of tenements on the lower side of the street, and two new houses on the corners of Warren and Monroe were erected, but it is doubtful if more than one or two others were built on this old part of the street. There can be no doubt in regard to the name of the street; no name of early patriots was more revered by Massachusetts soldiers than that of Warren, and the old Revolutionary men who lived on this "40 feet way," some at least were in the battle in which this talented young officer died.

Coming back to Merrimac street, the house on the upper corner of Dove is the one in which John Kent, son of the deacon lived, and is not less than 150 years old.

Geo. Burroughs bought this house in 1779, with the 2 1-2 acres of land through which he opened his "40 foot way," for 2100£ ($7000); in 1782, Burroughs sold the house and barn with 41 1-2 rods of land for 1836£ ($6120), to Collier. Dove street, two rods wide, was opened in 1795 or '96. The lot on the lower corner of Dove and Merrimac upon which the three story house stands had been sold in 1772 by Richard Kent to Michael Norton, 20 rods for 26£ 13s ($89). In 1799 Norton sold this land and the buildings to Samuel Rollins, and Rollins sold it the same year to Capt. Joseph Patch for $875, "bounded on the northwest by a two rod way" which was Dove lane.

In 1797 Mariner Kent sold Michael Norton 13 rods on Dove lane for $45.85, and in 1812 Norton sold 20 rods with buildings to James Dennis for $605, on "Dove lane." It is said that one of the old houses on this street has in its frame timber from the old church in Market square, which was taken down in 1801. House lots on this street were not so desirable as on the other new street and so there are few old houses upon it.

The land below the three story house on Merrimac street was bought from Kent by Thomas Merrill and the two houses there were probably built by him or by some of his family. The one now occupied by John Creedon was owned and occupied 70 years ago by "Aunt Hannah Merrill," the ancient school dame mentioned above. The house on the corner of Kent and Merrimac streets was the Somerby house; it was there in 1788 and when Kent street was laid out in 1788, the northwest side of the street started from this house. This concludes the sketch of all the old houses on the Kent land upon the upper side of Merrimac and between Kent and North streets.

There remains the lower side of Merrimac upon which were not only dwelling houses, but stores and manufacturing establishments. The lots upon the lower side of the street were different from the other lots as they bordered upon the river, and this gave them a commercial value different from the other lots.

Merrimac street from Kent's landing to Moody's lane was opened two rods wide by John and Richard Kent about 1750. The first lots sold were on the lower side of the street. The river being the great natural highway had a prospective value above that of the upland. In the river front above Kent's landing no reservation of "river lots" had been made by the old proprietors. Below Kent's the river front to Pearce's farm, South Green street, had been divided into 225 lots, Kent's landing originally was not as wide as now, and about 1710 it was enlarged probably by taking on lot 224. In 1728, Jonathan Woodman conveyed to his son, Jonathan, river lot 222, 24 feet, 6 inches wide, and in 1748 Henry Sewall conveyed to Henry Kingsbury, lot No. 223 for 44£ ($147.) Several landings were by tacit consent of the old proprietors left open for public use along the river upon Kent's property. One such landing was Pilsburys, in the rear of the old house that stood on Merrimac opposite the foot of North now Oakland Street.

In the course of time some of the public landing places became the dumping places for rubbish; one of these was the landing near the foot of Olive street, and in 1894, a petition was sent to the legislature and granted to allow the city to dispose of those landings for which there was no public use. Theoretically, the city had no legal claim to the ownership of these places, as the title was vested in the old proprietors, but practically and for the public good, and as no person could prove an ownership in them, the deed given by the city was valid as a warranty deed.

The lots then sold by John and Richard Kent included the flats as well as the upland.

The building next above Kent's landing was, a century ago, occupied by Butler Abbott, a leather dresser and wood pudder, and after his time by Henry Merrill, Jr., who did considerable business in that line. Abbott lived in the three story house on Kent street. In 1812 " Butler Abbott, tanner, bought of Michael Smith, merchant, the house and lot and a half rod of land for $1350." The house next to Abbott's tannery was moved to its present location about 30 years ago from land now occupied by the brick store house of the distillery.

Sixty years ago a two story carpenter's shop stood where this house now stands, occupied as a shop by Charles Pearson and George Towle, which was struck by lighting and burned. Near the brick store house 40 years ago stood the old house built by the first settler, Richard Kent, Senior. This old house was in the possession of the descendants of Richard, Sr. until after the death of Dea. John Kent. In 1803, it was owned by John Miltmore, who that year sold it to Alexander Caldwell with 50 rods of land for $2000. In whose possession it remained until redivided.

The house next above the brick store house was built probably by carpenter Gneenough, *sic* and the gambrel roof house opposite the foot of Dove street by Thomas Burroughs, the husband of Rebecca Kent. Burroughs bought the land for this house of Deacon John in 1762, and was married in 1766, so that the house was probably built as early as 1766.

The lot next to Burroughs was the first one sold on the "two rod way opened by John and Richard from Woodman's land to Moody's land and the lane in it." In 1753, they sold to Benjamin Kingsbury 29 rods of land for 46£ ($153.33). Kingsbury built the two story house recently occupied by Mr. Creeden, deceased, and in 1762 he sold to Rowell the "land and buildings" for 113£, $376.66. In 1789 Rowell sold to Corliss this lot "of upland with the flats adjoining, five rods on the highway; with two dwelling houses." The two houses were the two story one and the three story one next above it. This seems to indicate that this three story house was built by Rowell between 1762 and 1789. The property was owned in 1795 by John Corliss and Enoch Bradley and was sold by them in that year to Daniel Richards for 330£, $1100. Richards was a trader and in the small one story shop, now standing, transacted much business. He had a wharf at which small vessels discharged their cargoes. In 1841 the heirs of Richards sold the three story house, wharf and shop to True Sargent. In this shop Sargent had a grocery for many years. The three story house was occupied by him as a dwelling until his death.

Elbridge, the son of Mr. Sargent, changed the lower story of the house into a grocery store as it is now. In 1840, True Sargent had bought of Josiah Little the three story house next above the one story grocery for $500, the land measuring 140 feet on the street. This seems a small price for so much real estate, but at this time property could be bought for a fraction of its cost.

The next dwelling house on the lower side of the street was the one belonging to the estate of Joseph Williams with the one adjoining. The Williams' house was built by Captain Joseph Sevier about 1806, and the one above by Jonathan Merrill a few years after. The latter house passed into possession of Capt. Sevier and in 1825 his heirs, the four "Sevier girls" who lived on Kent street sold the property to Michael Pearson.

The house nearly opposite the foot of Tyng street is the old Choate house. In 1773, George Burroughs bought of Richard Kent the land for 23£ 6s, 8d, $77.78. The house was built by Burroughs and he, in

1782, sold the house and the land, 14 rods on the street, to George Searle for $900. In 1798 the widow of Searle sold the property to Jeptha Spaulding who opened it as a tavern. Spalding, before this time, had kept the toll house and tavern at Deer Island. In 1812, Ben Choate, ship-joiner, bought the estate of Spaulding, but it continued to be used as a tavern for some years. About 1827, Pottle Richardson kept it as a house of entertainment. Being on the road from Deer Island bridge to "town," which was a main line of travel, it was a convenient resting place for travelers, especially for those with teams from the country loaded with country produce, which they exchanged for imported goods. After the house ceased to be used as a tavern, Mr. Choate occupied it and passed the remainder of his life there. The great barn was used by him as a shop in which he and his sons with other skillful mechanics worked. In 1852 or '53, the old shop with a new one in front was burned. After Mr. Choates death his heirs sold the estate to the late Wm. Morse.

 The next house, known as the Gage house was built by Wm. Milbury upon land bought of Jeptha Spalding in 1798 and '99. In 1801, Milbury sold house and land to Jonathan Gage, a man afterwards of wealth, who owned the house on the corner of Green and Pleasant streets as well as other property. Capt. Gage had two daughters, one of whom, Sarah, was the wife of Capt. Wm. A. Cheney. In 1830 Gage's affairs became involved and the real estate was made over to Richard Stone. In 1844, Mr. Stone sold the house to Ben. Pickett, who for a few years was a ship builder at Belleville. After it passed out of Pickett's hands and through the hands of Nathaniel Hills, it became the property of Storey, who in 1867 sold it to Edward Cogswell. The gambrel roof home next to this was built about 1800 by Stephen Pilsbury upon the land sold to his ancestor, Samuel in 1773.

O. B. MERRILL

Fig. 1. Northeasterly view of Belleville area of Newburyport taken from the home of Capt. Charles Lunt, 6 Rawson Avenue. The Rawson Pilsbury house is in the foreground, circa 1890. *Collection of the Historical Society of Old Newbury.*

Fig. 2. Caldwell Distillery on Merrimac Street taken from the foot of Kent Street, circa 1900. No longer extant, it was located at 222 Merrimac Street. *Collection of the Historical Society of Old Newbury.*

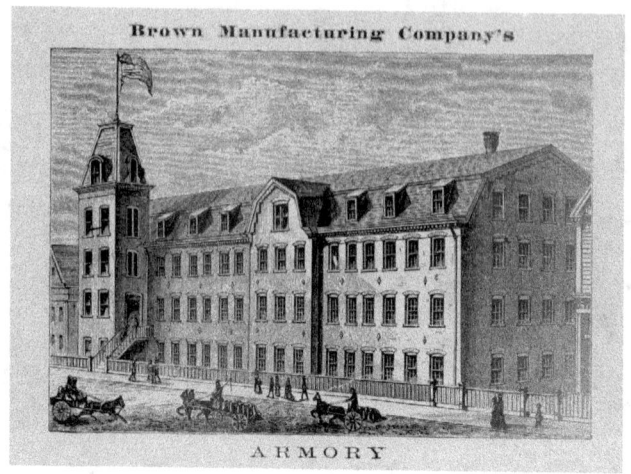

Fig. 3. Brown Manufacturing Company, 216 Merrimac Street in 1871, between Board and Tyng Streets. In 1880 it became the Towle Manufacturing Co. *Collection of the Historical Society of Old Newbury.*

Fig. 4. Federal home built by Thomas Coker at 44 Broad Street. *Collection of the Historical Society of Old Newbury.*

Fig. 5. "View Near the Laurels" looking downstream to Plum Island with the port of Newbury right center. *Collection of the Historical Society of Old Newbury.*

Fig. 6. Rawson Pilsbury house, 267 High Street. High Street is in the foreground, circa 1890. *Collection of the Historical Society of Old Newbury.*

Fig. 7. Market Square, the busy center of Newburyport, circa 1870. Photograph by H. P. Macintosh. *Collection of the Historical Society of Old Newbury.*

Fig. 8. 1876 drawing of undeveloped blocks of the Belleville area which today includes Payson, Magnolia and High Streets. View is from the steeple of the Belleville Church at 300 High Street. *Collection of the Historical Society of Old Newbury.*

Fig. 9. Panorama of the Belleville area of Newburyport's waterfront showing mixture of residential and commercial buildings. Towle Manufacturing Company and the tall stack of the Ocean Mill can be seen. Caldwell's Distillery is located in the center. Circa 1930. *Collection of the Historical Society of Old Newbury.*

Fig. 10. Panorama looking north toward Monroe Street, between Tyng and Broad Streets. The Towle Manufacturing Company appears near the river. Picture was taken from the Anna Jaques Hospital, circa 1900. *Collection of the Historical Society of Old Newbury.*

Fig. 11. Kent Street looking toward the Merrimac River, circa 1900. *Collection of the Historical Society of Old Newbury.*

Fig. 12. Curtis Hat Factory, 208 Merrimac Street showing the 1872 boiler explosion. *Collection of the Historical Society of Old Newbury.*

Fig. 13. Looking down Green Street from the Court House on the Mall. Original steeple of the old Baptist Church can be seen in the distance. Circa 1880. *Collection of the Historical Society of Old Newbury.*

Fig. 14. View from the foot of Green Street corner of Merrimac Street looking south toward Newburyport City Hall, circa 1890. *Collection of the Historical Society of Old Newbury.*

Fig. 15. The building of the schooners *Richard S. Spofford* and *Horace W. Macomber* at George E. Currier's shipyard at the foot of Ashland Street. 1890 Photograph by George E. Currier. *Collection of the Historical Society of Old Newbury.*

Fig. 16. The Macomber with keel in place having its inside planking laid. *Collection of the Historical Society of Old Newbury.*

Fig. 17. This building at 35-37 Kent Street was constructed in 1805 as a schoolhouse for boys and was in use for 50 years. In 1854 it was converted into a residence.

Fig. 18. This row of single family dwellings on the "Albert Currier block" at 15-29 Monroe Street was built in 1845-46 by Albert Currier for the Ocean Mill.

Fig 19. The home of Oliver B. Merrill at 38 Monroe Street was built by his father Robert M. Merrill about 1845

Fig. 20. The Bass-Whitney house at 26 Tyng Street was built in 1807 for Edward Bass, Jr. In 1858 the house was inherited by Thomas H. Whitney, a cousin.

Fig. 21. This house at 42 Broad Street was built by Thomas Coker circa 1800.

Fig. 22. The Benjamin Pilsbury house, located at 3-5 Broad Street, was built circa 1803 by Pilsbury when the North End was being developed as a residential area.

Fig. 23. This house, located at the corner of Eagle and Carter Streets, was built by Mr. Selfridge in 1850.

Fig. 24. The Abel Keyes house at 33-35 Carter Street, corner of Carter and Cutter Streets, was constructed about 1811. In 1867 the Ocean Mill acquired the property and it may have been used as a tenement for workers.

Fig 25. The Toppan-Whitney house, at 237 High Street, at the corner of Kent Street, was built by Enoch Toppan and his son Steven in 1804. The Kent Street façade is shown.

Fig. 26. This circa 1845 building was originally part of the Ocean Mill and was later converted to residences.

Fig. 27. The Toppan-Tyng house at 249 High Street was built circa 1799 by Steven Toppan and sold that year to Dudley Atkins Tyng.

NORTH END PAPERS. NO. 12

Newburyport Daily News, Saturday, August 11, 1906, p 5.

Industries, 1762 – 1840.

The manufacture of distilled liquor began in the town between 1760 and 1770 and continued to be a flourishing business for half a century. Several plants of this kind were started in 1765-66 and '67. In 1790 there were ten distilleries and in 1808, eight such concerns. In 1820 the number had decreased but the quantity of rum made had not diminished. In 1820, 3000 hogs heads of molasses were used and in 1826, 3600. About one-fifth of this was exported and the remainder used in this country. Large quantities of molasses were brought from the West Indies by vessels that went from the town freighted with the produce of the region for which the town was the natural outlet, and returned laden with West India goods. As the molasses was very cheap and the rum sold for a high price the business of distilling was very profitable.

Cushing's history says that about one-fifth of the product of the distilleries was exported. We are not to infer from this that the remaining four-fifths was used in town. Enough was used to make an immense amount of drunkenness as rum was a very common drink. An account of the building of a house costing $1600 – has the "rum bill" $32.00, which represented more than sixty gallons of New England, or a less quantity of West India rum. As Newburyport was a business center for a large country trade much of the fiery liquid went to the inland towns. Our own town, however, was not the only place where this business was carried on. In Boston and its vicinity, were many plants of the kind, and there were few places that had not heard of Medford rum and the "Striped Pig." Large quantities were exported; many barrels went to the coast of Africa to purchase slaves especially in the years in which the slave trade was allowed.

Of the distilleries in Newburyport a century ago more than half the number were located above Green street.

One was in the brick building at the foot of Carter street; one at the foot of Kent street on the upper side of Kent's landing; another on the lower side of the landing in the brick building now owned by the heirs of Littlefield; two more owned by the Williams' family in the buildings, one of which is used for a foundry and the other for a grocery; another on the corner of Merrimac street and the bridge road in the old store recently torn down, one on Winter street about 100 feet from Merrimac; still another on Brown's wharf owned by Moses Brown, and one on Washington street owned by Coker.

The North End papers are concerned only with three of these, first the one at the foot of Carter street. The business of distilling was a favorite investment with men of money, and as the same men invested in more than one of these concerns, the financial entanglement makes the history of these plants difficult to trace.

As nearly as can be traced from imperfect records, this plant and the one now owned by Caldwell Brothers seem to have been projected by a distiller named Andrew Nichols who in 1762, bought of Deacon John Kent for £64 -- $213, a lot of land on Merrimac street, 135 feet front, and in 1765 another lot of 40 rods, 66 feet on the street for £52. The first lot was near the foot of Carter street and the other opposite the foot of Kent street. In 1765 Joseph Somerby sold Joseph Remick for 235£ -- $776.33 thirty rods of land with the buildings, "the house being eight feet from the two rod way." In 1767 Remick sold this property to Moses Little and Beniah Young for 200£--666.66 bounded northwest by Andrew Nichols and southeast by Ben Kingsbury. Nichols probably became interested in the plant and his land became a part of the large lot upon which the brick building now stands was erected about 1767.

In 1774 William Nichols sold Moses Little, the land, distillery, buts, worm, vats.

In 1789 Little and Young sold or mortgaged the plant –"two acres of land with distil house," etc., to Thomas Thomas for $2823.

After 1780 its affairs were somewhat confused, and between 1789 and 1787 *sic* it came into the hands of parties named Price of Andover, who in 1787, mortgaged the "distill house, three copper stills, twenty butts," and other apparatus to Nathaniel Tracy for 450£--$1500. The sum of this mortgage shows that the amount of business done here was large. Price evidently was not successful as a distiller for in 1791 he was sued and judgment declared against him in the sum of 1107£, 13s, 4d -- $3692.22. In 1792 the property passed to Augustus and Louis Duinoussay of the Kingdom of France, but living in Maryland. A few years later it was owned by another Frenchman,

Jolin Juteau, who in 1798 sold it to Joseph Sevier and Jonathan Merrill, mariners.

The estate measure 200 feet on the street; was bounded on the northwest by land of Moses Brown and southeast by land of Thos. Thomas. It included the land upon which the brick distil house stood and also that upon which Mrs. Williams' house and the one above now stand. Soon after 1800, the Williams family came into possession if it, but their affairs for many years were so involved that it is hard to trace the ownership of the property. In 1811 an advertisement appears in the Herald of "one fourth part of the distillery, for sale, occupied by Joseph Williams."

In 1826 an advertisement appears of the "opening of the distillery formerly of Abraham Williams, first on the river road as you enter town from the bridge." A new establishment owned by John Chickering; purchasers supplied either by Chickering or by James Blood, agent at the distillery." The "river road" was Merrimac street and the bridge was Deer Island bridge. Chickering seems to have been the last distiller in this building; for in 1833 James Blood bought the distil house of Abraham and Wm. C. Williams for $2250.

Tradition says that Mr. Blood tried his hand at the business but with poor results, and that he sold the movable apparatus of the distillery for a goodly sum. Mr. Blood, however, used the vats for the manufacture of vinegar with which commodity he was successful.

The establishment owned by Messer's Caldwell is interesting from the fact that it has been in possession of the Caldwell family since 1772. As has been shown above Andrew Nichols, distiller bought of Deacon John Kent, 40 rods of land near the foot of Kent street. At some time between 1762 and 1765, Kent sold Wm. Coffin, mariner, and Joseph Sprague, distiller, land adjoining Nichols. In 1767 John and Richard Kent sold Coffin and Sprague more land and this same year, 1767, Coffin and Sprague mortgaged the "land with distillery, wharf, warehouse and distilling apparatus" to Patrick Tracy, for 1466£, 13s, 4d -- $4889. There is little doubt although it cannot be absolutely proved by the records, that this plant was started as early as 1765 probably by Nichols.

The evidence that it came into the hands of Caldwell although circumstantial, is conclusive. In 1772, Patrick Tracy bought of Kent a lot of land on Merrimac street, described as "being southeast of the distillery sold or to be sold to Alexander Caldwell." Now Tracy was the man who held the mortgage given by Coffin and Sprague and this statement would not have been made in this deed had it not been true. Again in 1772 Caldwell bought land, 95 1-2 feet front, bounded on the southeast by Patrick Tracy. As nothing appears about Coffin and Sprague after 1767 it is probable that they were not successful and that Caldwell took the mortgage.

There is no evidence that the Kent family had anything to do with distilling. Richard Kent, the first settler, was a maltser by trade, and find nothing on the records to show that he or any of his descendants had anything to do with distilling. When the old house was torn down, however, a deep and carefully constructed cellar was found evidently planned for keeping either distilled or fermented liquors. Perhaps he carried on his trade in the old house and used this cellar to ripen his beer, thus producing a kind of "lager."

The third distillery at the North End was on the lower side of Kent's landing. In 1774 Geo. Burroughs sold Wm. Morland a lot of land measuring about 100 feet on Merrimac street, upon which are now standing the brick building owned by the heirs of Littlefield and the three story house next below. In 1789 Morland sold to Wm. Caldwell one fourth part of a certain parcel of land "whereon are the brick still house now improved by myself and Caldwell." In 1796, Morland, Caldwell and John Knight sold Samuel Coffin for 900£ --$3000, the plant bounded N.E. by the river, northwest by a narrow strip – a water lot – owned by Cross, southeast by land of Cross and southwest 100 feet by Merrimac street, "with wharf, stores, and distillery, with stills, worms, pumps, etc., same as Geo. Burroughs sold to Moreland in 1774." When Caldwell bought one fourth of this plant in 1789 he paid 540£-- $1800, the whole being worth $7200. Samuel Coffin carried on the business here for several years.

In the year 1800 eight distilleries are named on the assessors' books – seven of which were above Green street. Merrill & Savier, at the foot of Carter street assessed for $1200; Alexander Caldwell at the foot of Kent street $1800; Sam Coffin next below Kent's Landing, $8500; Joseph Williams, Jr. at the foot of Strong street, $1700; Coffin and Otis, corner Merrimac street and Bridge road $5000; Moses Brown, distillery wharf and stores $10,000; Joshua Titcomb $1800, and one other at the lower part of the town owned by Sam Rolf, Benj. Wyatt and Israel Young $3600. As these are assessors' figures they are less than the true value and show that large sums were invested in this business.

The business of distilling seems to have been a favorite one with mariners, a possible explanation of which may be that the captain often owned his own distillery he saved expense. The presence of the sea captain in this business may explain a curious circumstance in regard to the vane that usually crowned the ventilator on the roof of the shed that covered the vats which was a fish.

The industries of the olden time were numerous but small. The factory system and the machine had not driven out the labor of the hand, and nearly everything manufactured depended on the skill of the workman and so, we find the carpenter, the cabinet maker, the cooper, the blacksmith, the shoemaker, and others each in his own small shop busy in supplying the wants of his community. The many trades with which ship building was concerned employed a large part of the men at the North end. The shipyards at Belleville were not often idle, and below Kent's landing ships were built, from 1676 nearly to 1840. Boat building was carried on extensively by the Pillsbury's and others. Probably few grocery stores of any account were in operation before the time of Sargent and Blood. Sargent opened his store before 1840 – and Blood about 1836 in which year we find his advertisement of West India goods and groceries, as well as Botanic medicines. In 1837, Blood took as partner John Tewksbury, an energetic young man who had kept a grocery store in the brick store owned by Littlefield next below Kent's landing. This partnership continued until 1842 when Tewksbury built the store at the foot of Woodland street, where he sold groceries for several years. He lived in the tenement connected with the store, but afterward built and occupied the cottage on North Atkinson street now owned and occupied by Obed W. Greaton.

O. B. MERRILL

NORTH END PAPERS. NO. 13

Newburyport Daily News, Saturday, August 18, 1906, p 5.

Richard Kent, Senior,
1634 – 1654

Among the settlers at Parker river were two men named Richard Kent. When the new town was laid out along the Merrimac river, Richard Kent, senior, set up his household at the foot of Kent street and thus became the pioneer settler in that part of the town. Richard Kent, junior, pitched his tent upon the island that bears his name. Richard, Jr. does not concern us except that his name must not be confounded with the North end Richard. Our pioneer deserves more notice than the meager records afford, and had not the Newbury settlers been men above the average of colonists in wealth, worth and intelligence, he might have been more prominent than he was.

Richard Kent was born in England and desiring to try his fortune in a place free from many of the tyrannical restraints that prevailed in the old country, he joined a company of men who were to emigrate to the new world under the authority of the Massachusetts company. In 1633, he took the oath of supremacy and allegiance which a man must take before being allowed to depart from the old country.

These two words "supremacy and allegiance" carried with themselves three centuries ago, a meaning of which the present generation has but a feeble conception. The fathers and grandfathers of Richard Kent and his companions had lived in times when a wrong conception of the meaning of these terms by the subject, meant the prison or the halter, "Supremacy" with Queen Elizabeth and with the Scotch pedant James, meant the claim under "divine right" of king or queen to rule the minds and consciences of men.

Queen Elizabeth's predecessor "Bloody Mary" lighted up the market place of Smithfield with burning heretics and the savage bishops of the "Virgin queen," who pretended to be ignorant of their infamous acts, were quite as cruel in a less spectacular manner. In all government, at this time church and state were one and the religious arm controlled and directed the secular power. In theory this might have been correct, but in practice it required the experience of free institutions in America to prove its fallacy. As the king or queen was in England the head of both church and state, it required no great stretch of construction to make a denial of supremacy, a denial of allegiance and this was treason, the punishment for which was to be hanged, drawn and quartered. In the time of Charles the first, from whom the charter of the Massachusetts colony was received, matters had softened a little as the forces that culminated with Cromwell and put an end to the divine right of kings, were gaining strength. The policy of the government was to keep the citizen at home.

And so having taken the oaths which would keep him from hatching treason in the distance wilderness in 1634, Kent set sail in "the good shippe Mary and John of London, Robert Sayres, master," and with 21 fellow passengers came to Ipswich in 1634, took the "freeman's" oath the same year and in 1635 came to Newbury.

The "freeman's" oath was the one by which he swore allegiance to the government of the colony. The officers of the colony took an oath of allegiance to the king as British subjects. This latter oath was of more importance than might at first seem, as it was to the king – not to the government. The charter of the Massachusetts colony came from the king, not from the Parliament, and so that during the years that proceeded the Revolution, the state claimed that it was an integral part of the British empire and not a dependent colony, that it had as much right to representation in the governing body as citizens who remained "at home," that numbering as they did nearly one third of the kingdom, the rest of the kingdom had no right to impose a tax upon them, by legislation in which they had no part. The men who obtained the charter from Charles had little confidence in him and so that document is very carefully worded. It is of great length and interesting from starting point of free institutions. The charter is found in the first volume of Mass. Colonial Records.

The law of the colony ordered settlers to keep together near the meeting house, but as they soon tired of close quarters they began to wander to other parts of the large town. Richard Kent was probably one of the stragglers who before the new town was laid out, in defiance of the law selected for himself the beautiful spot upon the banks of the great river, and on the borders of the primeval forest, set up his household goods. People of middle age can call to mind the old house that stood opposite the foot of Kent street in front of the distillery.

A century or more ago Merrimac street ran nearer the river than at present, the upper side being as far towards the water at least as the car track now is. The old house stood a rod or two behind an elm tree that is there now, and faced the south. It was a staunch, solid old house and after the sunshine and the storms of more than two centuries, it might have stood still longer had its place not been needed for other purposes. The old house was torn down more than thirty years ago to make room for the new brick storehouse.

In 1650 Goodman Kent gave up his lot at Parker river and received thirteen acres in the field beyond Mr. Rawson's, and six acres more. It is not easy to locate this tract of land with absolute certainty from the imperfect records, but there is little doubt that it was the lot upon which his house stood once, the land along the river as far at least as North street. Probably his house was built before the land was assigned him.

Probably some disaffection existed between Kent and the town authorities for in 1638 Kent and ten others petitioned the general court for leave to begin a plantation at Merrimac – that is on the north side of the river. Their petition was granted conditionally – "they were allowed to begin a plantation and have liberty to associate others * * * and if any difference fall out amongst the planters about the seat of their town or receiving of other associates or of allotment of lands, that then this court and the council shall not order it."

Probably Kent contemplated removing to the new settlement had the conditions been agreeable, but instead located, either with or without leave from his associate proprietors, on the spot where he built his house.

A natural curiosity on our part to see the scenery as Kent saw it more than two and a half centuries ago, need not depend wholly upon imagination. The Massachusetts company which received its charter in 1628 was anxious to develop its territory as rapidly as possible, and the English government – while, throwing many obstacles in the way of emigration – paradoxical as it may seem, was urging the settlement of plantations as far to the "eastward" as possible in order to keep the French from gaining a foot hold there.

The Massachusetts company in order to advertise its land employed a man to "write it up" somewhat after the style of modern promoters, and so William Wood wrote and published a remarkable circulation in the old country. The name of this book was "New England's Prospect," and it gave the first reliable account of this part of

America. Wood came to New England five or six years before the settlement of Newbury and lived at Lynn. He was a very bright and intelligent man and had traveled over the Massachusetts territories until he knew it very thoroughly. His book was published in 1634, and making some allowance for the "size" of his stories is a very valuable book. It was nearly out of print as to our times when Eben Moody Boynton in 1898, secured a copy and had it reprinted. From this book and from our old records as well as from the "lay of the land" we can form an idea of the surroundings of the old Kent house.

The spot selected by Goodman Kent for the location of his home was one that commanded an extensive view of the great river from the islands above to the ocean below. Free from the defilement and disorder that came with civilization, in its wild beauty it must have been attractive. From the ridge above the land sloped gently to the river with great oak trees here and there to the water edge. Spaces open to the sun were between the trees; here and there a broke [brook] ran to the river, draining the land above. In the open places exposed to the sun the Indians had planted "corne and isquowter, squashes," a fruit like a young pumpion." The trees were "greate oakes" centuries old; tall, straight pines, soon to be marked with the king's arrow, and more trees, says Wood were here. He also found many fruit trees in the forests – "plummes and cherries," of which latter fruit he says – "they so furred the mouth that the tongue will cleave to the roofe, and the throate wax horse with swallowing" – showing that the old historian had made the acquaintance of the choke cherry.

"In the great forests were found beares, deare, wolves, squerrills, rabbits, bever and wild cats, The beasts of offence," says Wood "be squnuskes, ferrets and foxes, Geese, ducks, partridges and pigeons, and turkies that would weight 40 pounds a piece were there. In the Merrimac were all kinds of fish, saammon and sturgeon 12, 14, 18 foot long, clammes, muscles and oisters."

We are not to imagine that the woods near Kent's house harbored all the beasts and birds that the historian tells about, or that all the kinds of trees were found there, but without doubt this region contained its share of the good things of nature. No human habitations before Kent were here unless perchance some hunter or trapper had built a hut for temporary shelter, or a hardy fisherman who drew from the rich treasures of the river, it means of profit and support. Wood in describing Agaman says "it is the best place but one which is Merrimac where is a river 20 leagues navigable."

While Goodman Kent had no neighbors above, he probably had such below him not many rods south of his house Mr. Edward Woodman placed his house which he occupied for several years if not for the greater part of his life which old house is still standing where it has stood more than two hundred years. Beyond at the foot of Olive street was the home of Wm. Titcomb, in an old house torn down in 1895. Across the river Robert Ring had set up his fishing house, where he prepared for market the sturgeon, salmon and bass with which the river abounded.

Kent was by profession a maltser, that is, manufacturer of beer, but whether he made it for sale is doubtful. Large quantities of beer were used as we use tea and coffee, especially until the appetite for stronger drink arose and the distilleries furnished their fiery stimulant. Kent was in the main a farmer, and in the pastures near by had his herds of cattle, sheep, goats and swine.

He raised on his plow land corn, wheat, barley and turnips for food, with flax for making of linen and hemp for sale to the rope makers. The woods were full of game that could be had for the taking, and the river abounded in fish easily taken. Thus we see that Goodman Kent with the resources, of the soil, the river and the forest, with his flock and herds and the imported goods that his surplus products purchased, must have been a prosperous member of the Puritan settlement. Richard Kent died in 1654, leaving a son John, and several daughters. His will is on file just as it was written with a grey goose quill more than two centuries ago; at first sight, beautiful to the eye with the flourishes of the old scrivener who wrote it, but as difficult to decipher as a page of cuneiform characters from a brick from the walls of Babylon.

John Kent received from his father, Richard, the house and land. In 1690 he sold to James Anderson, one acre and thirty rods for – 12 £, 5s— $40.83. This was a strip four or five rods wide and was probably between Kent and Carter streets and near it not a part of Monroe street. John Kent's will was dated 1703, and the inventory of his estate gives "Housing, out-housing, upland and meadow" valued at 283£, 13s, 4d—$945.57. Allowing for difference in the value of money, this would represent in our time about $5000 or $6000.

There seems some doubt as to line of descent in the third generation from Richard Senior – but in the fourth we find according to Joshua Coffin, John, afterwards deacon, born in 1690 and Richard born in 1710. No deed on record shows any change in the ownership of the land until it came into the possession of John and Richard. In 1761 Richard gave to John a quit claim of the old house and the land around it. Probably Deacon John lived here, and after his death the ownership of the old house passed to other hands. Before 1803 it was owned by John Miltiman and he in 1803 sold it to Alexander Caldwell, grandfather of the present owners of the land. The first white man then to claim ownership to the tract of land reaching from Kent to North street was Goodman Richard Kent Sr.

O. B. MERRILL

NORTH END PAPERS. NO. 14

Newburyport Daily News, Saturday, August 25, 1906, p 5.

Edward Woodman's Land, Kent, High and Monroe Sts.
1681 – 1845

The part of the North End territory remaining to be sketched is that between Kent street and the 20 acres of Archelaus Woodman bordering on High street for about 500 feet. This was a part of the estate of Edward Woodman assigned to him by the "lott layers" who laid out the new town.

In the early division of the upper field lot No. 41 was assigned to Edward and No. 42 to his brother Archelaus. It is difficult to tell whether the two lots were both on the lower side of the country road, or whether No. 41 was on the corner of Toppan lane. In 1681, Edward conveyed to his son, Jonathan Woodman, this land with other real estate. Jonathan by his will dated 1706 bequeathed this field of about eight acres to his son William, and in 1710-11 William sold four acres of it to his son Jonathan, Jr., 33£, $106 2-3, bounded southeast by Woodman's lane; southwest by the country road and northwest by Geo. Marsh, "on the nineteenth yeare of the reign of our soveigne Lady Anne, of Great Britain, France and Ireland Queen."

In 1685, Jonathan Woodman had sold to Geo. Marsh a strip of land 57 rods long, 12 1-2 rods on High street and 5 1-2 rods at the lower end. This lot was between the 20 acres of Archelaus Woodman and that sold to Jonathan, Jr. No deed appears on record of a conveyance of this land to any one from Marsh, but other deeds show that it came back to the Woodman family.

Between 1710 and 1811 many changes took place in the ownership of this land which are difficult to trace except in a general manner. In 1745 Abigail Woodman sold to Hilton Woodman for 70£, $233 1-3 old tenor, the lot that had been owned by March *sic* with some more land on the southeast. In 1757 Hilton Woodman sold this to Joseph Rowell for 42£, 13s, 4d, $142.25. After this the land from Kent to the present Carter street was divided into several long and narrow strips probably for the purpose of a land boom in 1767. Rowell sold

Nathaniel Carter a strip 45 rods long and 7 1-8 rods wide for 61£, 13 s, 4d, $205.50. Between this and High street was a strip owned by Montgomery and below Carter's was another, purchased by John Boardman while the part through which Monroe streets extends was owned by Sylvanus Plumer. In 1788, Carter bought a part of Montgomery's land. These sales took place about the time when the 20 acres of Archelaus Adams came into the market and when the Kents were selling lots on the lower side of Merrimac street.

After 1767, many changes took place in the ownership of this land. In 1804 John Greenleaf sold to Richard Pike and others four acres, twelve rods, extending from Kent 31 rods or about two-thirds the distance from Kent to Carter street, for the sum of $2250. Some time after 1804, says a deed, Pike laid out Eagle street about two-thirds its present length. A deed given in 1812 speaks of "said street as laid out to Lloyd street." In 1811 Carter street, called Lloyd street at first; then Keyes and because it ended at the old Keyes house and finally by the city named Carter street was opened. Wm. Smith, who owned the field on the northwest side, gave a strip half the width of the three rod street, while Josiah Smith, David Coffin, Richard Pike and the heirs of Boardman gave the land for the southeast half of the street. Sylvanus Plumer owned the land from Carter to Kent and he gave the land which joined Carter to Warren, thus making a continuous street from High to Merrimac.

Seventeen lots were laid out upon Eagle and Lloyd streets and several were sold but not for building purposes.

The first house built on High street between Kent and Carter was by Moses Cheney. In 1784, Cheney bought of Thomas Coker for 30£, $100, twenty rods of land, bounded southeast by Ben. Coffin, northeast by Sarah Woodman and northwest by John Tracy. In 1793, Cheney bought of Coker 40 rods on the southeast of his first lot, and on a part of this lot he built his house. In 1800 Cheney sold 25 rods of this land to Levi Swain, and in 1803, he sold the rest of the land to Moses Lewis "with the house 18 feet by 38 feet, two stories on front with a one story linter in the rear." The "linter" was a lean-to or an ell with a shed not.

As the house now occupying the site is three stories in height and much larger on the ground, it is evident that the present house was not the Cheney house unless perchance it has been built over and enlarged. In 1872 Albert Currier sold the house to Mr. Dimmick.

The house next to the Cheney house was built by Levi Swain about 1800. A few years later Swain sold the house to Jonathan Chase, and he in 1810 sold it to Dr. John Bond, who mortgaged it to Swain and probably did not redeem it. In 1817 Swain sold the house to David Wood and in 1819, David Wood, 2nd bought it of the heirs of Abner Wood; in 1843 David Wood, 2nd, sold it to Chase and in 1855 Capt. John Borarus became the owner of it and lived there until his death.

The large brick house on the corner of Kent and High was built by Enoch Toppan and his son Stephen, and was intended to be a costly house. An advertisement in the Herald in May, 1804 offers for sale 40 rods of land on the northwest corner of Kent and High streets. This land was owned by the heirs of Richard Pike and was bought in 1804 by Enoch Toppan. In 1807, Toppan bought of David Coffin a strip of land on the northeast of his lot "on a new street" which was Eagle street. The house was built and finished between 1804 and 1808, probably occupying three or four years in building. The evidence that it was built about this time is found in an old account book. This bill for painting is given in full to show the cost of such work a century ago:

To painting brick house inside 61 yards at 4 cents, once over.
To painting do 868 yards, twice over at 8 cents.
To painting 362 yards walls at 3 cents.
To setting 14 lights of glass at 6 cents.
These charges were for the labor.

The price of stock was for oil, $1.38 a gallon; spirits $1.33; white lead 22 cents a pound; blue paint 25 cents; yellow 21; green 50; putty 15 cents a pound; litharge 25 cents. These pigments came to the painter dry and generally had to be ground in a stone mill. A charge of about three cents a pound was made for grinding. For painting sashes the charge was a cent a light and for painting blinds 8 shillings a pair. In the brick house the walls of some of the rooms were painted. The building of this house was a costly venture for the Toppans and resulted in financial loss to them. Attempts were made to sell it without success and so it was rented until 1837, when the heirs of Enoch Toppan sold it to Wm. Ashby for a sum much below its original cost.

In 1811 the land along Monroe street belonging to Sylvanus Plumer was divided into lots and sold principally to Enoch and Stephen Toppan. Monroe street from Warren to Kent was opened between 1811 and 1830 from Carter to Broad in 1840; from Broad to Tyng in

1841 and from Tyng to North in 1848. Eagle street which had no houses was cultivated as field land by the owners of lots. A farm gate painted red, opened into it from Kent street, and the master of the North school used to warn his boys not to stray away at recess farther than the "red gate."

The beginning of the year 1845 found the "lay of the land" almost exactly as it had been for more than thirty years. The field bounded by High, Carter, Monroe and Kent had on it only the three houses, described above. The land below Kent to Buck had on High street only two houses, one the "Newtonian Institute of Parson Wilbur," a building with large columns in front, now standing on Buck street, and the cottage also owned by Wilbur now occupied by Mr. Choate and Mr. Ingalls. On Congress street were two wooden school houses and an engine house. The remainder of this field was used as a gravel pit. The hollow in the rear of the houses on Washington street was made by the removal of many loads of gravel for mending roads. The large field next below this bounded by Buck, Congress, High and Olive had on it two houses on High, three on Buck, one on Congress and one on Olive. The field bounded by Olive, Washington, Boardman and High had four old houses on High and a barn on Olive street. Thus it will be seen that nearly all the land from Broad street to Boardman and from High to Washington, Congress and Monroe was field land until after 1840. After the building of the Ocean mill in 1845, the land above Kent street was gradually improved, but below Kent there was little change until after 1860.

Upon this land no house was built on High street until 1847 when Horace Bickford, Esq., bought a lot of 24 rods for $285 next below the estate of the late John Balch. Upon this lot Bickford built a very beautiful and attractive cottage which he himself occupied. Some years later Bickford bought more land and built an addition to his cottage; so utterly unlike the cottage itself as to excite much remark. After Bickford died the property changed hands; the cottage was moved to its present location, and the "addition" remodeled was made into a one house which was finally purchased by Mr. John Balch.

The house now occupied by Dr. Hurd was built by Harrison Smart and his after *sic* and was occupied by them and their heirs until it came into the possession of its present owners. The houses on Kent street at between the Ashby house and the mill buildings are all modern houses, the first being built by Moses Quimby about 1855 or '56 and the others later.

North End paper, No. 15, will treat principally of the Ocean mill and No. 16 which will complete the sketch of the houses and land between Kent, High, Oakland streets, and the river, will tell of the more recent industries.

O.B. MERRILL

NORTH END PAPERS. NO. 15

Newburyport Daily News, Saturday, September 1, 1906, p 5.

The Ocean Mills.

Between the years 1815 and 1840 it is doubtful if more than two or three houses were built at the North End. In 1843 the land between North and Tyng streets was offered for sale and two cottage houses were built on North street – one by Josiah Sawyer and the other by John Atwood. On the Tyng street side, Mr. James Merrow built the house next above the three story Waterman house; Capt. Abram Somerby and Mr. Ballou, the one next below the three story house, and Benj. Dutton the one below Capt. Babson's. Other houses were built on the lot later. Soon after the opening of this land, the field owned by the heirs of Moses Brown between Tyng and Broad was offered for sale in house lots. The first houses erected here on the Tyng side were by Parsons Ordway and Thomas Atwood, and a small building was moved here by a son of Jacob Hale and made into a house. On the Broad street side no house was built until after 1850.

The development of the territory between Monroe and High streets began with the building of the Ocean mill.

Previous to 1845 on this whole tract of land reaching from High street to about 100 feet below Monroe street, the only houses were the three on High street – the one on the corner of Kent and Monroe occupied by Thomas Cutter, the cottage house on Dove street, built by Mr. Currier and the house on Warren street owned and occupied by Jacob Hale who kept a stove store on Merrimac street where F.E. Cutter and son now have a paint shop. The land was field land used by Mr. Ashe as pasture, and tillage land.

In 1845 the cotton industry had become well established in the town – the success of such business having been shown at Lowell and Amesbury – the new city of Lawrence being in the future. Lowell and Amesbury depended chiefly upon water power, but in our own town steam had to be used. The first mill built here was of wood and stood upon the wharf where the National Biscuit Co.'s building now stands. It was built in 1834. The first building for the Bartlett on Pleasant street was built in 1843 [In Paper No. 16, the date of the first Bartlett mill should have been 1837] and a second factory later, the two extending from Pleasant to Merrimac streets.

The James mill on Charles street in 1842, the Globe on Federal street with the Ocean on Monroe street in 1845.

The Ocean mill was incorporated by the legislature in 1845, Ben. Saunders, Wm. C. Balch, Edward S. Lesley with their associates and successors being the corporation. The capital stock was to be $200,000, and they could hold real estate worth $50,000.

The land for the factory was bought of the heirs of Rev. James Morse – from Kent street to Lloyd or Carter street, 10 chains, 34 links or 682 feet, and 5 chains, 35 links or 352 feet on Carter street. A condition of this purchase was that a new street be laid out by the heirs of Morse; this was done and the street called Ocean street. The land of which this was a part had been bought by Mrs. Morse in 1815 for $2000 of Richard Pike. It reached from Monroe to Eagle street. The mill corporation used for their buildings only the part between Kent and Warren streets, the part between Warren and Carter being sold to Albert Currier for the erection of the brick block, and the part from the rear of the block to Ocean street, to other parties.

The plan of the mill was made by Col. Fred Coffin, the work of building was carried on by Albert Currier for the mason work and Fred and Emery Gomn for the carpenter work, while the looms were built by Leslie. The Ocean was the smallest of the brick mills, and Mr. Currier was building the great factory of the Globe mill, 320 feet long at the same time as the Ocean – quite a business undertaking for a young man only twenty-six years of age.

The principal building of the Ocean mill was on Monroe street and was about 160 feet in length. On the middle of the front was a tower with a graceful belfry and spire surmounted by vane – the highest in town and most reliable then as now in telling the direction of the wind.

In the rear was the boiler house while the engine was in the westerly end of the first floor of the mill, and the whirl of the great fly wheel was visible from the street. On Kent street was the small counting room, and some distance above on the corner of Ocean street was the cotton house; on Ocean street was the blacksmith shop and near by the coal shed, the whole premises being enclosed by a tight board fence. Not the least importance if not in size of the buildings was the dog house where a big dog was kept to assist the watchman in his nightly duties.

The factory buildings and the large yard were kept in repair and in good order, and instead of being an ugly and unsightly mess—as many more modern factories are apt to be,--was a neat and attractive estate.

The first "agent" as the manager was called, was Benj. Saunders, who served in that capacity until 1855, when Edward S. Leslie took charge of things and continued until 1871. Mr. Lesley was a very ingenious machinist who in the early forties had a shop on Merrimac street opposite the foot of Winter and next to No. 1 engine house, where he manufactured many things in his line. His shop with the engine house was burned in 1843 or '44, and he afterwards occupied the brick building on the lower corner of Market and Merrimac street.

In 1867 the capital stock of the mill was increased to $300,000, and the new part of the mill on Monroe street built. This was a very unfortunate move for the company resulting in heavy financial loss.

Before the building of the new part the company was in a good financial condition with a considerable surplus. The completion of the new part was delayed a long time by the failure of the party that was to furnish the machinery. The result was that in 1871 the mill was sold for $209,600 by John Gardner, Geo. Gardner, Jos. B. Morse and John H. Spring for the old company.

The lot measured 425 feet on Monroe street, and the length of the mill on Monroe street 330 feet. A slight change of the name was made on the incorporation of the new company; the name "Ocean Steam Mills" becoming the "Ocean mills." The new company employed as agent Mr. Cumnock, a Scotchman, trained to the business of cotton manufacture by practical experience. Under his management a successful business was done. While here Mr. Cumnock lived on Broad street in the house now owned by Mr. Pilbrick. The old company in 1867 had bought several houses, namely the Keyes house and the three double tenement houses opposite the mill built and owned by James Blood, but these were for factory boarding houses. The president of the new company was Mr. Tucker, and the treasurer, Mr. Busn *sic*. The capital was $310,000. 75 men and 275 women were employed as operatives. The goods manufactured were sheeting and print cloth – that is cloth to be made into calico.

In 1874, A.D. Chandler became agent or manager, a man thoroughly acquainted with the business and a man of remarkable energy. At this time the company was reorganized, and strenuous efforts were made to do a successful business. Many changes were made in the plant to adapt it to more modern methods. New and powerful boilers were put in; the original square chimney was taken down and a round one built 100 feet high; new spinning and weaving apparatus replaced the old, and many minor changes made to meet the competition which was continually going on in the business.

In 1878, the plant again changed owners and "the Ocean mills" was sold to "the Ocean Mill Co." for $105,000. In order to increase its business capacity, the company determined to increase its working capacity by building a new mill. The old company in 1845 had bought land only as far as Ocean street, but the new company had bought the lot on the upper side of Ocean street and thus owned the land on both sides of this street except the part on Kent street owned by Mr. Dennett.

As more room was needed for the placing of the new mill, the city government was asked to close the part of Ocean street running from Kent to Warren. In March, 1880 the petition was granted and as the land on a closed street reverts to the abutters the company thus gained possession of this part of the street except the part abutting against Mr. Dennett's lot on Kent street. Upon this land the larger mill number two was built.

The new mill was built more in accordance with modern plans than the old building, being less in height, but of greater width. In 1884, a change again took place in the organization of the company and Joseph Wattlos took the place of Chandler as agent and manager, and Wm. Gray, Jr., became treasurer.

In 1886 the mill property again changed hands and became "the Whitefield *sic* mill." Why this name was used is a mystery unless invoking the name of the great evangelist was expected to bring better fortune to the enterprise.

Seth Milliken of New York was president and Stephen Greene treasurer and manager. Mr. Greene was a skilled mill engineer and knew how to plan and build a mill, but was not a practical manufacturer of cotton goods. The chimney 100 feet high by Greene's order was built to its present height of 166 or 158 *sic* feet so as to make sufficient draft for the furnaces. After the chimney was completed the men who built it celebrated the construction of their work with a clam chowder eaten on this breezy height.

The plant in 1886 had become very costly. In 1883, it had been assessed $120,000 for its real estate and $150,000 for personal; in 1888, the real estate was $145,000 and personal $118,000, the price paid by the Whitefield Co., was $175,000, or less than two-thirds the assessed value of the plant.

Naturally enough this company was not successful and after about three years came to an end. In 1889 the machinery was taken out and sent away, and the end of this company was the end of cotton manufacturing in this part of the city. The "whirr of the spindle, the clatter of the loom and the early warning of the bell" were heard no more at the North End. After being without an occupant for several years, the mill on Monroe street became a prosperous shoe factory and mill No. 2 a cordage plant with other temporary industries.

The Ocean mill from 1845 to 1889 was not on the whole a success. Large sums of money were sunk in it, to the extent of hundreds of thousands, but the query might easily be made whether any of the six great mills was a financial success. The capital of the Essex in 1834 was $100,000; of the Bartlett in 1837, $350,000; the James, 1842, $250,000; the Globe, 1845, $320,000 and the Ocean in 1845 $200,000 an aggregate of more than a million dollars. Two of these mills were burned – the Essex and the Bartlett and it has been said that these were the only mills in which the stockholders received the value of their stock – from the insurance, of course.

The reasons for the failure of these mills is not plain. The owners of the stock in general were men of good business capacity, but competition in this kind of business was very keen. The management of the industry itself throughout New England was to a considerable degree lacking in economy. It was said that once some English manufacturers, visiting Fall River had remarked that at home they would be satisfied with profits equal to the waste in New England mills. One item of expense was the large number of paid officials. The English manufacturer was his own buyer, selling agent and manager – while in this country the pay of such officials was a heavy tax upon the financial part of the concern. For the business community, however, the mills were a valuable industry. In 1850, when they were all running, more than 1300 operatives were employed and more than 10,000,000 yards of cloth were made.

The building of the Ocean mills in 1845 led to the erection of new houses and the fixing up of many old ones for tenement and boarding houses. Mr. Currier built the brick block which furnished good tenements and James Blood built three double tenements opposite the mill. Between 1850 and 1860 houses were built on the upper side of Kent street; upon Ocean and Carter streets, but not many upon Eagle street until after 1860 and none at all upon the upper side of Carter street until after 1866.

O.B. MERRILL

NORTH END PAPERS. NO. 16

Newburyport Daily News, September 8, 1906, p 7.

1840 – 1880.
Arms, Brush, Hat and Collar Factories, etc.

Stores and manufactories – some large others small, have flourished for a long or short time along Merrimac street. The store at the foot of Kent street, now occupied by Creeden was built by Luther Merrill upon land leased from John Caldwell, Sr. Chesley and Merrill kept a grocery store here for many years and John Caldwell, Jr., carried on the same business here. The grocery formerly owned by Mr. Sargent, is no doubt the oldest of any at the North End – tracing its origin back to Dan Richards, more than a century ago.

The store at the foot of Broad street was built by E.M. Reed in 1851 or '52 and has been continued as a grocery since that time.

Many small grocery stores have been run for a short time, as also other small shops for the convenience of the public.

At the foot of Oakland street in the old yard where the Pilsbury's for several generations had built boats was the shipyard where Eben Manson and his partners built vessels from 1851 to about 1873. More than thirty vessels were built here from the little schooner of 40 tons to the great ship of 1320 tons, amounting to more than 10,000 tons.

At the foot of Tyng street Wm. Morse about forty years ago built a shop on the site of Choate's old joiner shop where he constructed wherries. Since Mr. Morse's death the same business has been successfully carried on by Gideon Webster.

The land upon which the silver factory stands is a part of the original tract assigned to Richard Kent, Sr. before 1650. It passed to his descendants, but was not for sale until the time of John and Richard Kent about a century after the death of the old pioneer. By John and Richard it was sold to Patrick Tracy soon after the opening of "the two rod way from Woodman's lane to Moody's land, and the land there," – not long after 1750. From Mr. Tracy it passed to Moses Brown soon after 1780. The lot measured about two acres and extended from the Choate property to the three story house owned and occupied by Michael Pearson. It remained in possession of Mr. Brown and his heirs until 1850 when Mrs. Sarah W. Hale sold the land, 330 rods, 105 feet on the street to Warren Dockham and others for $1000. In 1852 the legislature gave leave to Dockham to build a wharf to extend 1070 feet from Merrimac street—the wharf to be of piles beyond 720 feet from the line of the street. Mr. Dockham and his associates thought this to be a good location for an extensive business and so the wharf was built as well as several buildings on the southeast part of the lot. The expected business, however, did not come and in a few years the project was abandoned after the expenditure of much hard labor and a considerable sum of money.

In 1859, the property was sold to Henry W. Moulton and he in 1859 sold to E.M. Reed all the land except that between the present limit of the silver factory estate and the three story house below. Mr. Reed had previously bought in 1851 a lot 62 feet on the street, to which he moved a small blacksmith shop where he stored flour. In 1866 Mr. Reed sold the land for $1550 to E.P. Bray, Edwin Blood and Geo. Merrill, who conveyed it to the corporation known as the "Merrimac Arms and Manufacturing Company." In the Newburyport Herald of July 21st, 1866, was an editorial in which were set forth in glowing terms the great advantage that would accrue to the business interests of the city, could a certain company of skilled mechanics be induced to locate here and manufacture certain goods under valuable patents which they held. This company had been located, or was thinking of locating in the city of Worcester. It claimed to have a capital of $150,000, but wished to increase this to $200,000. This company held possession of the valuable patent of the Ballard rifle as well as of a machine for carving. It was willing to locate here if $50,000 could be raised to increase the capital to $200,000. Were this condition complied with, the company would build a factory 100 feet long, 40 feet wide and three stories high in which they would manufacture guns, pistols, and various other things in their line of business. The offer was a tempting one; the money was raised; the company took the name of "The Merrimac Arms and Manufacturing Company," and in the summer of 1866 built the factory at the foot of Broad on Merrimac street. The real basis of the concern was the Ballard rifle. The managers were Mr. Ballard, Mr. Merwin and Mr. E. P. Bray, who lived for while at the Woodland cottage.

This company brought into the city a class of very skillful and ingenious mechanics, and for a short time did business that attracted much attention. As the tenement houses at the North End were not quite equal to the wants of the new comers the company leased several good houses and bought of Mr. Henry Merrill two houses on Merrimac street.

In 1867 the property was mortgaged to Bray, Merrill and Graves for $25,000, which mortgage was foreclosed and the plant sold to Charles S. Brown. The building was enlarged by adding a tower on the upper end of the building. Brown, held the patent for the "Van Colt," – rifle said to be a highly improved firearm. A few of these rifles were made at the factory as specimens of the new arm, at a considerable cost.

The makers of these rifles expected to receive large contracts from the United States as well from foreign governments, but their specimen guns failed to pass the tests required and so were not a success. After this the company went along for a few years and finally about 1873 collapsed entirely.

The original building was not devoid of architectural beauty. It was two stories in height of brick, with a third story of wood in the form of a mansard roof; the entrance was in the middle of the front and was reached by a flight of steps. In Mr. Currier's History of Newburyport, on page 172, is an excellent picture of the factory as it was in 1905. A little exercise of the imagination will enable one to see the building as it was in 1866 by leaving off the tower and the part beyond and placing the steps with the entrance door in the arched projection of the front. Some years after the passing of the Arms Co. the building was fitted with machinery for spinning cotton, and was afterwards used by various small industries, being idle much of the time until 1883 when it was bought by the Towle Manufacturing Co.

In 1863 a private concern known as the brush factory was started in a wooden building opposite the foot of Broad street. Its capital was $30,000 and it was expected to manufacture brushes of various kinds.

The parties concerned in it were H.W. Moulton, the owner of the building with Edwin Blood and others. The capital was $30,000, and this was the first of the North End business concerns that belonged to the period of the war. The requisite machinery was put in, a stock of material purchased and the plant started with a fair prospect of success.

In 1865 needing more money the factory was mortgaged to the Institution for Savings, and after running until December, 1866, it was sold at auction for $10,000. A new company was incorporated in 1867 with Capt. Wm. Graves, president and John N. Pike, treasurer, with a capital $18,000. After running about three years and manufacturing goods at a loss, the brush factory came to an end. The building was afterwards used as tenements and stores of various kinds and was finally burned. The building now standing on the site, is an entirely new one built by Mr. Atkinson.

The three story house once owned by Michael Pearson was sold to Mr. Dresser and the lower part converted into stores which have been used for various purposes. The front part of the Williams house was converted into a drug store by the late Joseph Williams.

A short distance below was a two story building, burned in 1905, used as a brass foundry, carpenters shop and meat store.

In 1840 the old distillery in which Mr. Blood had his grocery store was essentially of the same appearance as it had been in the time of Young and Little. In front on the street was the head house, a one story building running back 30 or 40 feet; in the rear of this on the low ground was a long shed with brick walls in which were distillery vats. No change was made in the building until a demand arose for tenements after the Ocean mill was built. Mr. Blood then raised the roof over the store and made two tenements there. No further changes were made in the building until 1864, when a proposition was made to start a hat factory at the North End. Mr. Blood with his son, Edwin, invested in the concern, and to furnish a factory Mr. Blood altered the old building into its present form by raising the walls of the shed on the rear, and placing a boiler house on the northwest side. Here the Essex hat company with William Cushing as president and Edwin Blood as treasurer and agent began operations as manufacturers of wool hats with a capital of $100,000. For some reason this company was not successful, and in 1869 it gave place to the Curtis hat factory, a new concern which was run with prospects of success until 1872 when an unfortunate accident brought the business to an end. From 1880 to 1883 the Towle Manufacturing company occupied the building and in 1885 and 1886 Mr. Read manufactured tooth brushes there. Afterward it was used as a bakery and finally in 1905 or 1906 passed into possession of its present owner.

In the Herald of March 28, 1866, the optimistic editor has an editorial in which he hints that something is coming in the industrial line that will be a blessing to the city and of course a good pot into which spare greenbacks may be dropped. In the course of time this new project came to light with the name of the "American Machine Company" which was to manufacture paper collars as well as the machinery used in that industry. The capital was to be $30,000. There were in operation in other parts of New England 10 or 11 such establishments, all of which were doing a good business, as paper collars were very generally in use and an immense number of them were manufactured. In some way this industry appealed to the community as something sure to pay and the stock was taken very largely in the neighborhood by people who had from $100 to $300 of savings to invest. A wooden building three stories high was built for the company on Merrimac street near the foot of Warren, by James Blood.

The company started with much promise, but soon came to a halt, through an attempt on their part to use a new kind of machinery that had not been tested as to its profitable use. The usual way of cutting the collars had been by a die which had a vertical up and down movement. The new machine consisted of two cylinders which were worked with a rotary motion, and were much more rapid in action than the older ones, but as the styles of collars were not permanent and changed with fashion, the form of the cutter had to be changed, and with the new machine this was a costly matter. Several of these machines were made after much delay, but for lack of experience in the use of them, the operators failed to succeed. Dissatisfaction and disagreement arose among the managers and stockholders, and the industry which, under judicious management would have been prosperous, came to an end.

After the building was vacated by the collar company various small industries occupied it temporarily and in 1872 the shoe firm of John D. Pike and Horace Choate converted it into a shoe factory and used it until 1881. It was afterwards used as a box factory for a time but was many years without a tenant. It was finally sold to the fair association and taken down, the material being used for the erection of the sheds, etc. on the fair grounds of Grasshopper Plains.

The question may well be asked why these four business concerns of considerable magnitudes were failures.

The answer is found in the financial conditions that prevailed during and after the war. A depreciated currency was a condition that the country had known little about since the days of the revolution, and the effect was to cause a feverish and unhealthy excitement in business affairs. This was especially true of manufacturing. People rushed into all sorts of schemes without reference, and with a reckless management that reached its natural result. Thousands of dollars were lost in the North End factories by individuals and large sums by the savings banks.

This paper closes the series of papers giving a sketch of the development of a part of the old town of Newburyport. The purpose was to trace the ownership of the land from the first owners of the soil down to modern time, and to give the history of the substantial and solidly build houses that have stood the sunshine and storms of more than a century, and are good for the use of many generations yet to come.

In paper No. 15 the date of the building of the first Bartlett mill should have been 1837 not 1842.

O. B. MERRILL

NORTH END PAPERS. NO. 17

Newburyport Daily News, Saturday, January 18, 1908

Woodman's Lane and Kent Street.

1800—1854

Along the banks of the Merrimac river the dried-up beds of many small streams can be traced which drained the forest land upon which the city stands. Several such brooks, some large, others small, found their way into the river between ash swamp—above Ashland street and Market square. One such brook which drained a large territory between Woodland and Ashland streets with the fields on the upper side of High street, was flowing in historic times, that is, within a century and a half. Its Indian name was Mopan or Mowpan.

The main part of this brook was up on Woodland street: at the foot of that street the alluvial formation of the soil seems to show that it spread out and found its way into the river by several outlets.

The fact that this was a natural water course shows the reason why Woodland street was so often injured by great floods of water, beyond the capacity of any cobble stone gutter to control. Here it may [be] said that by the ingenious device of dividing the flood by underground drains, its force has been placed under control.

When the trenches for the sewer pipe were opened in ward six in 1901 the workman found near the foot of Woodland street large stones, which had been placed in the bed of the old brook. Merrimac street from Kent's landing to Moody's lane, now Woodland street, was opened two rods wide by Dea. John and Richard Kent as early as 1753, and was without doubt continued to Poore's lane on Merrimac court to afford approach to the shipyards and incidentally to the old ferry at Carr's island, so that these stepping stones must have been placed here at an early date.

At the foot of Broad and Tyng streets the great number of springs, as well as the formation of the soil, show that a brook was here which flowed into the river a few rods above the silver factory.

The brook however, with which the subject of this paper is concerned, ceased to flow before Old Newbury was settled. It drained the land between Kent and Olive streets from the river to High street, as well as the high land to the summit of the Ridge. It carried a great volume of water and many tons of silt to the landing at which it found its way into the Merrimac and tore out of the earth a gully that reaches from Russia street to Merrimac. This natural landmark must have attracted the attention of "ye lott layers" whose duty it was to divide the common lands among the early settlers, and it was made the dividing line between the land of Edward Woodman on the lower side and of Richard Kent Sr., on the upper. It also formed the lower part of the old road known for more than a century as Woodman's lane.

Woodman's lane was a long, crooked, straggling road, varying in width from two rods to four. It started from the river and ran between Mr. Creeden's store and the house below, through the gully, to Russia street, where it bent around to the South and ran to the country road on High street; using a part of the country road it extended down Toppan's lane and across the pasture to Aspen swamp and Turkey hill. From the river for more than half a mile it ran past land owned by Edward Woodman or his brother Archelaus. The most interesting part of the old lane was the lower part, because it ran, says an old deed, on the backside of the house of Edward Woodman.

The lower part of the lane was not parallel to the lower part of Kent street but ran into the upper part of Woodman lane which was the same as Kent street, about where the old brick schoolhouse now stands on the corner of Russia and Kent streets. The land on the Northwest side of the lane was owned by the Kents and was well situated for building purposes, while the sides of the old lane were entirely unfit. The land owned by the Kents extended nearly to Congress street, and no doubt a lane ran through it in early times, but not until 1788 was the town willing to accept the new street and discontinue a corresponding part of the old lane. The new street was to be three rods wide. Merrimac street at this time was only two rods wide and its upper side was about where the car track now is [1908]. The land on the lower corner of the new street was owned by Abel Kent and his house, which was afterwards moved to its present site next above Creeden's store, stood on this corner. The lower side of the new street started from a stone at the corner of Abel Kent's land and ran S. 60° W. thirty eight rods to a stone wall. The upper side started from a tree at the East corner of the Somerby house which is still standing, the house not the tree; and ran thirty-six rods and eleven links to a well in front of Mrs. Sawyer's house. This house is still standing and is owned by the heirs of Geo. Pearson. It was modernized by the late Charles Pearson, about sixty years ago. The well in front was closed a few years since. Abel Kent's house was sold by him in 1795 to Jonathan Mason for £240 or $800, and Mason sold it to Capt. Wm. Orne for £275 or $883.50. It was afterwards sold to Mr. Haskell and when the land was needed for widening Merrimac street in 1834 it was moved to its present location and made a two tenement house.

House lots on the new street sold readily. On the lower side Wm. Toppan Mason bought a lot; in 1796 David Cooper bought 23.6 rods for £49.11s or $155.16s; John Tufts, blacksmith, 21 1-6 rods for £31.15s or $115.87, and in 1812 Butler Abbot bought of Michael Smith, merchant, the three story house and 10 1-2 rods of land for $1350.

Abbott was a wool puller, leather dresser and tanner. His shop stood and now stands, just above Kent's landing. As all the meat used in town was from animals slaughtered by resident butchers, there were plenty of hides, not only for Abbott but for other tanners. On the upper corner of Russia and Kent was an old house owned in 1774 by the widow Foster, later by Peter Gilbert and sixty years ago by Mr. Coffin. In one of the front rooms of this house Mrs. Coffin kept a little shop where she sold to the boys who attended school in the school house opposite, pencils, paper, striped candy, peppermints on a narrow strip of paper, as well as hard, but toothsome dainty known as a gibralter *sic*.

On the upper side of Kent street the first lot sold was in 1788 to Capt. Joseph Sevier, house and land for £107.10s or $358.32s. This house was occupied for many years by the "Sevier Girls," the daughters of Capt. Joseph; it is now modernized and owned by Mr. Charles W. Blake. Houses were built soon after the year 1800 by John Bailey, Capt. Morrison and others. The oldest house upon the street is the one formerly owned by Wm. L. Dodge. In 1690 John Kent sold to James Anderton or Anderson, one acre and thirty rods, of land for £12.50s or $40.83 on the West side of Woodman's lane. Upon this Anderton built a part at least of this house. In 1738 Anderton made over to his son James this property, receiving the use of the house to himself and his wife during their lives. Some years later it was owned by John Butler, and sold by him to Moses Davis, who in 1831, conveyed it to Wm. Cross surveyor in the Custom House. In 1835 Ruth and Mary, daughters of Major Cross sold it to Wm. L. Dodge.

On the assessors' book for 1800 we find taxed for real estate on Kent street, Dr. Wm. B. Leonard, Edward Edwards, Ab. Mace, Nath. Plumer, Simeon Pearson, Benj. Pearson, Capt. Sevier, Sam Shaw, Wm. Toppan, John Tufts and others.

The first public building at the North End was built upon Kent street in 1805. The population at this part of the town had increased to such numbers, that need arose for a school house, the nearest temple of learning being at the West end of the Mall where a crowd of boys were packed into a small wooden building. Several private schools had been supported by the people, taught by wandering pedagogues, one such by John Ewing, kept in a room near the foot of the street, while "dames" schools were in the summer provided by the town for the small children. The demand was for a writing school which in a measure corresponded to a modern grammar school. A vote was passed by the town to build a brick school house one story high after the style of the one at the East end of the Mall, built in 1796. The building was begun, but when the walls reached the height at which the roof was to go on, the people thought that two stories would be better than one and the result was the only two story school house in town. It had a tower upon Russia street, and a belfry surmounted by a spire upon whose top was a quill for a vane. In the tower was a bell, brought by some sea captain from a foreign land, probably plundered from some church or plantation. On the rim of the old bell was an inscription in French, which has puzzled antiquarians. In this building the North male grammar school was kept until 1854, when it was declared unsafe and abandoned for school uses. The first master of the school in 1805 was Wm. Popkins; then Robert Harvey in 1807. Dan Easkell in 1815, Geo. Rogers in 1817, H. Wheeler and C.W. Milton to 1820, Nathan Brown in 1820, Josiah Bartlett in 1823, Geo. Titcomb in 1835, Joseph Williams in 1840 and E.G. French in 1845. The old bell after many wanderings now rests, rusty and forlorn upon the roof of the engine house in Ward 6. The school for boys was kept in the lower story of the brick school house until 1841. In 1812 three new schools for girls were started, one of which was placed in the upper story of the Kent street building. These were called in 1812 "Girls Grammar Schools." The teachers of the Kent street school were Miss S.J. Moulton, 1812 to 1816; E.A. Lunt to 1817: M.S. Coolidge to 1831: Mary Tappan in 1832: Priscilla Titcomb 1833 to 1835: Ellen Swett to 1838: E. Titcomb to 1839. Soon after the school was moved to the new building on the corner of Buck and Congress street.

O.B. MERRILL

NORTH END PAPERS. NO. 18

Newburyport Daily News, Saturday, January 27, 1908

The Pioneers—Woodman Farm—Custom House.

1650 to 1850

Between Congress street and the river many houses are now standing that were built a century or more ago. Most of these were humble homes, occupied by men of moderate means, but some are fine specimens of the style of architecture of their time. Solid substantial and costly they were the dwelling places of families of wealth, influence and social standing.

This part of the town of old Newbury and after 1764 of the town of Newburyport, is in one respect the most interesting of any section of the North End. It was here that one of the most eminent of the original settlers passed the greater part of a long and useful life. Edward Woodman was prominent in all town affairs, but is especially noted for being leader in a contest with the ministers which involved the churches and the courts and stirred up a storm that shook the very foundation of the Bay colony. This quarrel which was indirectly connected with the theocracy that controlled the colony was not on account of religious dogma but upon the question whether the pulpit or the pew should control certain processes in church government.

The real principle involved was, on Mr. Woodman's side, the germ of democracy; on the side of the ministers the divine right to command, and for the people dutifully, to obey. As account of this affair, covers more than 40 pages of Joshua Coffin's History of Newbury, but is treated more clearly in Mr. Currier's History of Newbury.

In another respect this territory is interesting to students of local history as it was here in this pleasant spot that the development began when more than two and one half centuries ago Mr. Woodman, Richard Kent, senior and Mr. Titcomb, set up their homes in the forest by the banks of the Merrimac and became the pioneers of civilization in this section of old Newbury.

The original homesteads of Kent and Titcomb were standing within the memory of the present generation. The old Kent house was removed about 30 years or more ago to make room for new buildings at the distillery and Titcomb's at the foot of Olive street was torn down in 1895. Woodman's farm reached from the river to Congress street and from Woodman's lane nearly to Olive street. He owned many acres of land in other parts of Newbury, but this with several acres on the upper side of Kent street was the homestead where he set out an orchard and raised "corn, wheate and barley for malt." His neighbors were the Kents and Titcombs nearby, with the Pillsburys, Toppans, Sewalls and his brother Archelaus more remote.

When the new town of Newbury was laid out by the Merrimac river about 1644, Mr. Woodman was assigned a lot of 40 acres on the corner of High and Toppan streets upon which he built a house and barn. He was also assigned the lot by the river. [not read-able] common land. There appears no evidence in the records that any one owned this lot before him. Woodman's lane for a half mile ran past land owned by Edward or his brother Archelaus. In 1650 Mr. Woodman sold his lot on Toppan's lane with the house and barn to Henry Sewall, whose daughter became in 1670 the wife of Jacob Toppan, the first owner of the old Toppan house. Naturally Mr. Woodman vacated the premises in 1650. Where would he be more likely to go than to the pleasant lot by the riverside? That he did do this seems plain from a deed dated 1681, which at that date speaks of orchards, plow land, and pastures, as well as crops of wheat, Indian corn and barley for malt, and a dairy producing butter and cheese. A farm in such a highly productive condition must have been started many years before 1681, and give reason to think that in 1681 Mr. Woodman must have lived here many years previous to that date.

The first deed on record in regard to this farm, is one in which Mr. Woodman conveys it to his son, Jonathan and is dated 1681. Mr. Woodman was at this time advanced in age and wary with labors of an active life as well as disappointed in his brave struggle for liberty and so to be relieved of the strain, he makes over to his son, his real estate under certain conditions. In the Ipswich registry, in Book IV, page 425 this deed is found on the old book where it was written two and a quarter centuries ago. Omitting a lot of legal verbiage it reads as follows: To all Christain people xx know yee that the said Woodman for natural and fatherly love and affection that I have and beare unto my sone Jonathan Woodman, xx and also for a consideration of 20 pounds to be paid in butter and wheate and fowel (fuel) [fowl] and chease and Indian corne and malt, which is yearly so to be payed during the lifetime of my owne and my wife's natural life xx do sell my now dwelling house and barnes, orchards and pasture, and all my plow land lying by and adjoining to the streets lyeing upon the westward side of my house, and all my plow land upon the North west side of the s'd streets being vulgarly called the "new streets." "The new street" was Woodman's lane now Kent street. "The Plow land" was on the upper side of Kent street from High to below Monroe street, the word "vulgarly" is here used in its old meaning of commonly.

   The conditions of this conveyance were that his father and mother should be supported by the son during the remainder of their lives. The sum of 20 pounds represented many times that amount in modern money and paid in products of the farm gave the old people a liberal support. Probably something else as well as love and affection had to do with the deed of gift. Jonathan was a ship builder and was in financial straits and the gift of the estate was doubtless to help his credit. This seems probable from the fact that soon after receiving the property he found himself unable to pay the 20 pounds and mortgaged the estate. This mortgage was paid in 1697 and [the] lease gives the bounds of the seven acres upon which Mr. Woodman's house stood, "North East by ye river Merrimack; South East by land of Mr. Titcomb; South West by land of Isaac Bayley and North West by ye lane commonly called Mr. Woodman's lane."

   No record tells us the date of Mr. Woodman's death nor does anyone know where he was buried, but the part that he took in the pioneer work of the old town will always be a monument to his memory.

   Jonathan Woodman was a ship builder and had a shipyard below Kent's landing. The later years of his life were passed in Haverhill and his will dated 1706 was made there. In the inventory of his real estate we find one house and most of the land received from his father. No record appears in the registry of deeds to show that Jonathan had sold the house that Edward owned and occupied in 1681. After sundry bequests to others, Jonathan in his will leaves the remainder of his property to his son, Ichabod. Ichabod had a son named Lewis, and in 1777 Lewis sold to Wm. Caldwell and he to Alexander Caldwell for £400--$1333. 1-3, the land and buildings on the corner of Merrimac street and Merrill lane "once owned and occupied by my father Ichabod," says the deed. This leaves little doubt that the "now dwelling house" of 1681 stood here. Mr.

Caldwell some years later removed the old house and built the large and costly house now there.

The oldest house now standing on Woodman's farm is the rear part of the three story house directly opposite Kent's Landing. The lot of an acre, was bought by Wm. Moulton, a part in 1724 of Ichabod Woodman and the remaining part, of his widow in 1727, the price paid being £105 14s--$353.33. Upon this lot Moulton probably built the house now standing. Nothing seems known about him except that he was a "trader." He lived but a few years and in 1730 his widow, Sarah sold the land with house and barn to Henry Kingsbury for £250 or $833. Kingsbury was a mariner and his wife, Rebecca was the daughter of Capt. John Kent who lived in the old Kent house. Kingsbury had several sons, one of whom John was a shipwright and probably built vessels in Jonathan Woodman's shipyard. Henry bought land above his house in 1735 and built the house at the head of Caldwell's court, which in 1747, he conveyed to his son John. After the death of Henry, his son John sold in 1762 to Ralph Cross, Jr., half an acre of land with two houses, on the corner of Woodman's Lane and Merrimac street for £333. 6s or $1111. These were the two dwelling houses now standing there. In 1789 Ralph Cross sold to Wm. Cross these houses with one and a half acres of land for £505 or $1683.33.

Ralph Cross, Jr., and Wm. Cross were both men of note. They were shipwrights by trade. Ralph owned the old shipyard of Jonathan Woodman near the foot of Merrill street, which he sold to Wm. Cross in 1789. No doubt many vessels were built here. Ralph Jr., was prominent in the Revolutionary times. He was a member of the committee of safety, chosen by the town in 1774, and in 1775 when the town was divided into four districts for training the militia, he was made captain of the fourth district, extending from Market street to the North boundary of the town. Major William Cross was captain of a company of artillery in 1792, and in 1794 commanded a battalion. He was for many years an officer of the custom house.

In 1826, James Prince was collector; William Cross surveyor; Thos. Carter, naval officer and Solomon H. Currier deputy collector. The duties collected in 1826 amounted to $49,966; the imports to $166,811 and the exports to [$]190,720. The present custom house was built in 1835. The old house bought of Kingsbury by Ralph Cross was remodeled extensively by him or by Major William. A three story front was built on to the old house, planned evidently by some carpenter who knew little about the fitness of things on architecture. As the passion for building this style of house here did not prevail until after the old house came into the possession of the Major in 1789, it is possible that the changes were made by him.

In 1833, Ruth and Mary Cross, daughters of William, sold to John Bradbury for $1500, "about one and a half acres of land with dwelling house and buildings, being the same dwelling house, garden and outhouses, occupied by Sr. Wm. Cross during his lifetime," being bounded northeast by Merrimac street; southeast by John Calwell *sic;* southwest by heirs of Butler Abbott, and Northwest by Capt. Wm. Orne, Wm. Toppan, David Cooper and DeFord." The initial "Sr." in this deed means surveyor, the office in the custom house filed by Major Cross. Mr. Bradbury occupied the old house until the time of gold excitement in California and is said to have been one of the voyagers to that Eldorado. The old house soon after passed to the Caldwell family.

The house on Merrimac street on the upper side of Caldwell's court was built by John Brown, glazier, who in 1732 bought the land of Sarah Moulton. In 1748, Brown sold to Jacob Toppan for £60 old tenor, thirty rods of land above the house. Afterwards the house was owned by Toppan and in 1780 Eliza Toppan sold to William and Alexander Caldwell the house and sixty rods of land.

All the land and houses from Merrill street to Woodman's Lane and from Merrimac street to Cross' land came into possession of the Caldwell family who occupied portions of it for many years.

O.B. MERRILL

NORTH END PAPERS. NO. 19

Newburyport Daily News, Saturday, February 3, 1908

Merrill and Elm Streets.

1735 to 1812

Two lanes afterwards called Merrill street and Elm street were opened through the farm of Edward Woodman. No record tells when these old ways were opened, but deeds of real estate enable us to approximate to the dates of their opening as the land was sold for house lots many years before these lanes were accepted by the town and dignified with the title of streets. Merrill was opened between 1743 and 1751. At this time no lane was open from Merrimac street between Woodman's lane and Woodland street, in fact Merrimac street itself was not opened until about 1753 when John and Richard Kent opened "a two rod way from Woodman's lane to Moody's land and the lane there."

About this time a demand for house lots arose and Elizabeth Woodman who owned a large part of the land through which the new lane would pass saw an opportunity to convert her field land into town lots. That the lane was not open in 1743, is proven by a deed in which Mrs. Woodman, the widow of Ichabod, the son of Jonathan, conveys to her son Ichabod, a lot of land the eastern boundary of which was land of Benj. Pike. Now Pike's land was on the lower side of the future lane, and had the lane been open by 1743, it would have been the eastern boundary of Ichabod's lot. In 1751, Mrs. Woodman sold Sam. Toppan a lot on the lower side of a way thirty-one feet wide. In 1752 a lot was sold to Moses Merrill on the lower side of a way twenty-nine feet wide. These deeds show that the lane was open as early as 1751, although the width was somewhat indefinite. In 1757 Mrs. Woodman sold Daniel Pike two lots on the southeast side of the lane—one of 11 the other of 12 rods.

After the lane had been open more than twenty years, and lots had been sold upon which houses had been built, a demand naturally arose that the lane be accepted by the town, and called by an authorized name, and so on the petition of Moses Merrill, Moses Woodman and others the street was accepted in 1774 and given a name. In volume one page 222 of the town book, is found a plan of the street drawn by some person who had little idea of exactness, as no compass directions are given and the distances are not according to a correct scale. It gives, however, valuable information in regard to the laying out of the street in 1774. As laid out it varied in width, the widest part running southwest from Merrimac street being only 27 feet, and the narrow part now Russia street only 19 feet wide. At the junction with Merrimac street the old Pike house on the lower corner, stretched out into the new street; on the upper corner was Ichabod Woodman's old house with a well in the sidewalk. Between these two obstructions the "mouth" of the street was very narrow, only about 18 feet.

On the upper side the street was straight; on the lower side not straight on the lower part. From Merrimac it ran to Russia street, where it turned at a right angle and ran through to Woodman's lane, 19 feet in width. The street also ran southwest from Russia street towards the present Congress street about fifty feet, to reach a house of Thos. P. Merrill. Moses Merrill's house stood and now stands on the upper side of Russia street near the corner of Merrill.

The house lots sold before 1774 were on the lower side of the street but after the street was accepted by the town. Moses Woodman and others, children of Ichabod, sold Ralph Cross, Jr. for £74, 7s, 2d or $247.86, 263 rods of land on Merrill and Russia streets. Cross bought this land for speculation; probably his selling price was too high as no lots on it were sold until after 1800, the first lot on the corner of Russia street being sold to Capt. Joseph Babson in 1803. The same day Capt. Witham bought the lot adjoining. Each captain built upon his lot a gambrel roof house and on the boundary between their lots they dug a well.

The large lot below Capt. Witham was bought later by a Mr. Moore a teamster. Mr. Moore owned the house afterwards owned by Wm. H. Huse and his stable converted into a dwelling house was owned and occupied by N.A. Moulton. Capt. Witham's house was sold to Dr. David J. Merrill who occupied it for many years.

In the early days many sea faring men lived on this street whose experiences would be interesting were their records existing. They were at sea during the years when the great powers of Europe were hostile to our commerce. One such old captain was Joseph Babson, usually styled the commodore, whose adventures would make an interesting story had not some dirt pursuing housekeeper more than three score years ago "renovated" the attic of the captain's house and destroyed a chestfull of old documents that now would be priceless.

Capt. Babson was born in Gloucester in 1756. As he was old enough to follow the sea when the Revolutionary war began he [was] doing his duty in the extemporized [torn] the time. Capt. Babson was at [torn] during the time when many Newburyport vessels were taken by English and the French. His vessel was captured and taken to one of the West India Islands. The captain and crew were put in jail, but having no desire to remain there, the captain and a fellow officer dug out through the walls of the prison and escaped. It was said that the wife of [the keeper] of the jail assisted his escape by disguising him with a suit of the keeper's clothes and walking with him to a vessel upon which he escaped to his own land. Capt. Babson was personally acquainted with President Thomas Jefferson and when his [torn] voyages led him near the presence of the great Democrat he was sure [to be] welcome. Tradition say that during the Embargo, he had command of one of Jefferson's gunboats [torn] which he got the title of "commodore."

During the war of 1812 the valent captain tried his hand at privateering. The privateer *Salisbury*, was built at Salisbury Point, and with a strong crew from Salisbury and Newburyport, one of whom was Capt. Babson, sailed for the Bay of Fundy, cut off vessels bringing supplied to the British Army. Going ashore to a little landing on their own accord the Blue Noses were too much for them. One man was killed and others "skedaddled" to their vessel [and] made their way home. The *Salisbury* made no more patriotic trips but was bought by Capt. Babson and used as a freighter along the coast.

Capt. Babson first owned and occupied the house on the upper corner of Merrill and Russia streets, most of his life was passed in the house built on the lot bought of [Cross] in 1803 where he died in 1843. In the front yard of this house stood a pear tree which bore pears of large size utterly unfit to eat raw, but a valuable accessory to a boiled dinner. The tree became noted and many trees were grafted from it. The part of Russia street from Merrill to Olive seems to have been opened between 1810 and 1812. In 1781 Gabez Sanborn bought of M.C. Little for £[   ] or $190 in gold and silver, 23.5 rods of land upon Merrill street. Upon the lot Sanborn built the house on the corner of Russia and Merrill streets. In 1782 Sanborn sold half this house to Capt. Joseph Babson and the other half to Elisha Gurney. In [1 torn] Gurney sold Wm. Pickett a lot of land upon which the street was afterwards opened, reserving to himself "the right of way from his front door to the street" (probably Olive street until the new street was laid out. Wm. Pickett built the house on the corner of Olive and Russia streets, and Captain Joseph Pickett, the three story house on Russia street. No explanation has ever been given of the name of the street which was originally a part of Merrill street, but possible reason for this name is, that when the other nations in Europe were hostile to our commerce Russia allowed our vessels to enter some of her ports. It is not improbable that this street upon, or on which many seamen lived was thus named in grateful remembrance of this kindness.

Upon a poll tax list nearly a century old are found the names of the residents upon Merrill street. Jeremiah Burnham in the house was Thos. P. Merrill; John Hancock, 1812 master of the Schooner Sally, owned by Moses Brown; Sam. Creasey, [B torn er]; John P. Hazen— Mason worker with Dodge in 1808 on the new Baptist meeting house (Liberty street); Wm. Porter in the house with [Mo torn] Quimby; Nath. Towle, joiner, brother to Jabes and others. On the assessors book for 1800 real estate is taxes to Jos. Babson $300; Francis Creasy $400; Sam Curtis $300; Thos. Merrill, land $100; and Nathan Plummer house and land on Kent and Merrill (Russia) street $600. So much for this old street, the old houses in general are there yet, but not more than one or two are occupied by even the remotest descendants of their original owners.

On the upper corner of Merrimac and Elm streets where O'Neill's new building stands, an old house stood which was owned by Jonathan Woodman and was by his will given to his daughter, Hannah Nesbit, together with a considerable tract of land extending from Titcomb's land on the easterly side about half way to Merrill street on the westerly side. Jonathan, by his will allows his daughter Hannah, the use of one end of his dwelling house as long as she remains unmarried. This was not the house referred to above but was the one occupied by Ichabod, son of Jonathan.

In 1735, Hannah sold this right to Elizabeth Woodman who lived in the old house sold to the Caldwells in 1777. Eliz. Woodman was the widow of Ichabod, son of Jonathan, and the transfer by Hannah to Elizabeth is strong argument for the claim that the "new dwelling hose"of Edward Woodman stood on the upper corner of Merrimac and Elm streets. In that year Hannah conveyed to Sarah Butler "three-quarters of an acre, and half a quarter of land with dwelling house, barn and outhouses, etc."

The land around this old house was mostly owned in 1758 by Benj. Pidgeon and John Butler in 17[torn] gave a quit claim deed to Pidgeon of the house, barn and twenty eight rods of land, on a "drift way laid down for the convenience of John Butler and others." This is the first mention of the opening of Ash lane. In 1783 this drift way was evidently improved by John Butler and called in a deed of 1773, "a lane laid out by me to Merrimac river." A deed of 1794 calls the way Ash Lane.

The nearness of Ash Lane to the many small industries that were carried on along the river side, made it a desirable location for the homes occupied by mechanics. The old newspapers have advertisements for houses for sale or to let on Ash Lane. In old records are found the names of old families who lived here, Butler, Davis, Bradbury, Page, Merrill, Greenough and others. In 17 [torn] Benj. Pidgeon sold to James Merrill for £80 or $266.66, 16 1-2 rods of land on the corner of Merrimac street and Ash lane upon which the house now there was built by Merrill. In 1806 we find this house advertised for sale—"nearly opposite Major Cross's shipyard" says the advertisement.

The houses built here were cheap structures and the names of those who occupied them of no special note except as they help to show the development of the North End of the old town. No record appears to show that the lane was accepted by the town, nor do we know when its name was changed from Ash Lane to Elm street, but on the Assessors Book of 1835 it is called Elm street.

O.B. MERRILL

NORTH END PAPERS. NO. 20

Newburyport Daily News, Saturday, February 8, 1908

Between the Landings.

1676 to 1850

Between the landings means in North End papers, the land between Kent's landing and the one at the foot of Merrill street, now occupied by Mr. Donahue's store which was a part of the farm of Edward Woodman. When the new town of Newbury was laid out along the banks of the Merrimac, the proprietors evidently were in doubt as to the best way to grant the "lotts" on the immediate margin of the river. The banks of the river with its background of timber made it an ideal place for building vessels and so the assignment of these lots to private owners was not hurried. In 1704-5 a division was made of the narrow strip along the river, or on the flats from South Green street to Woodman's lane.

As the river was a great natural highway, numerous openings were left for public use, called "landings." The "River Lotts" were 225 in number and numbers 223 and 222 were next to Kent's landing. Kent's landing was at the foot of Woodman's lane and was a means by which people who lived on the higher land could reach the river.

This landing being flat and easy of access for scows from the river and carts from the land was much used. In 1763 it was enlarged from four rods to six by an exchange with Captain John Kent of 30 feet on the upper side for a corresponding amount of land on the lower side thus making this landing about 100 feet in width. The landing at the foot of Merrill street was much less convenient, the surface of the land alone making it somewhat difficult of direct approach. This landing had become in modern times such an unsightly place that in 1894 on the petition of the city government, the legislature allowed it to be sold. Mr. Donahue's fine store has converted an unsightly nuisance into beauty and order.

The tract of land between these two buildings was from colonial times for more than a century and a half the scene of active business, the most interesting being that of the old shipyard where vessels were built with more or less frequency from Jonathan Woodman's ship *Salamanda* before 1676 to Wm. Cross' Brig. *Rapid* in 1823. In 1835 Henry Merrill owned the shipyard, but whether it was used as such we do not know. Mr. Merrill owned the three story house next below the landing and had purchased the land above.

As to the ownership of the territory between the landing, we find in the will of Ichabod, the son of Jonathan Woodman, the shipbuilder, dated 1725, that he owned one-third of the wharf and warehouse inherited from his father. In 1728 Jonathan, son of the shipbuilder, sold to his son Jonathan river lot number 222, and in 1748 Henry Sewall, Jr. sold to Henry Kingsbury lot 223 for £44 or $146.66, in 1749 "Sam Plumer weaver, Sam and Benjamin Coffin, shipwrights: Cutting Noyes, joyner; Theophilus Bradbury coaster; Abigail Woodman and Joanna Knowlton, spinsters for £400 or $13,334, old tenor, sold to John Kingsbury six-ninths of the river lots of Jonathan Woodman mariner." As Kingsbury already owned a part of these lots this purchase made him possessor of all the land between the landings. The price paid being in a depreciated paper currency we cannot tell what the real value was.

In 1762 John Kingsbury sold Ralph Cross, Jr., a river lot 24 feet front joining a landing at the foot of Woodman's lane, also the warehouse on said lot. In 1789 "Ralph Cross sold to Wm. Cross a river lot of 170 feet bounded northwest by Wm. Moreland, southeast by a two rod landing and southwest by Merrimac street." In 1799 Ralph sold to Wm. Cross the river lot bought of John Kingsbury. The old shipyard then, extended from the Merrill street landing about as far up Merrimac street as the large three-story house now standing.

Some time before 1773, George Burroughs had bought the land from Cross' river lot, 24 feet wide, down Merrimac street to include the land upon which the three story house stands, and upon it, probably about 1765, built the brick building now standing and started a distillery plant. In 1773 Burroughs mortgaged it to Wm. Moreland and in 1789 Moreland sold to Wm. Caldwell one-fourth part of the land "with the brick still house now improved by myself and Caldwell," says the deed of conveyance. The price paid for this fourth part was £540 or $1800, the whole plant being worth $7200, showing that the manufacturer of rum was a very profitable business as far as money was concerned. In 1796 Moreland Caldwell and John Knight sold to Samuel Coffin for $3000 the land bounded northeast by the river, northwest by a narrow strip (the river lot owned by Cross), southeast by land of Cross, and southwest by Merrimac street about 100 feet "with wharf stores and distillery, with still worms, pumps and etc., same as Geo. Burroughs sold to Moreland in 1774." The sale of this concern in 1796 for less than its value in 1789 shows that Moreland and his partner had not made a success of it. Coffin, however, carried on the business and in 1800 his plant was taxed for $3500.

The large three story house on this lot was without doubt built by Coffin between 1796 and 1800. On the assessors' book for 1800 this house is taxed to Coffin at a valuation of $2400,.while the house of Alexander Caldwell on the opposite side of Merrimac street was assessed for $2000. Coffin was a merchant and shipper and transacted much business at his wharf and storehouse. The wharf extended out into the river and is said to have been called the Upper long wharf. Some other wharf down stream may have been called by this name before Coffin's was built. Many vessels lay at this wharf for sale or charter, and when there was danger of a war with France a vessel fitted with guns was offered for sale by Coffin. After the death of Coffin the property, except a part of the house, was sole to Capt. Eliphalet Brown in 1821, and from him Solomon Littlefield, teamster, in 1844, bought the brick store and wharf, while the three story house passed into the possession of Major Ebenezer Bradbury, a man prominent for many years in town affairs.

The most interesting feature of this space between the "Landings" is the fact that here a ship was built more than 230 years ago, the only craft of which we find an account fixing such an industry on the south bank of the Merrimac at the early date. Strange to tell, this piece of valuable historical knowledge comes to us through a court record, in which a crooked financial deal on the part either of the builder or the owner of the ship resulted in a law suit before the admiralty court of the Bay colony. It is often happens that good comes out of evil, and in this matter we should have no knowledge of the shipbuilder, Jonathan Woodman nor of his shipyard nor of his building the ship, except for the court records of the suit. Mr. Currier in collecting material for his "Ould Newbury" found this record on file at the State house and it is given on page 276 of that valuable and interesting book.

From the record it appears that the owners of the ship named the "Salamander" refused to pay a part of the cost of her construction, and Mr. Woodman entered suit against them. King Charles II was His

Majesty then and in his name the marshal or his deputy was ordered to summon into court Bartholomew Stratton, master and part owner of the ship, with the other owners to answer to Mr. Woodman's charge of refusing to pay the balance due him for building the vessel. Mr. Woodman complained that their refusal to meet their obligations had cost him in money and goods no less than £168, 17 s, 6d. In New England currency this equaled nearly $900 but as money then had a very different value from now this probably represented several times that amount.

When the suit was tried Jonathan not only lost his case as far as his demand against the owners was concerned, but was also fined by the court. The owners complained that the vessel had not been launched at the time agreed. Woodman replied that two carpenters upon whose work he had depended had been taken away from their work on the vessel; that he had been compelled to take up the deck and place it four feet heigher, and that he had been compelled to pay the owners £20 on account of the delay in launching. The owners complained that the vessel had not been surveyed according to the Province law; Woodman replied that she had been measured by the carpenters before being planked, in the usual manner. Jonathan's defense availed him nothing, and he was fined £10 for ignorance or neglect of the law. This fine, however, was remitted later. Whether Jonathan was brilliant intellectually either in financial or other matters may be questioned. He was one of the witnesses against old Goody Morse, who was accused of witchcraft in 1681. Jonathan testified that he saw "a catt and threw at it and it vanished" and the next day Dr. Dole was called to dress a bruise upon Mrs. Morse's head. Whether the "cat" came from Market street or from Market square is a question upon which historians differ.

It is probable that few changes were made upon the territory between the landings until after 1830. The brick store house became a grocery store and an addition to the rear furnished a convenient tenement for Mr. Littlefield. Below the three story house a small building was built in which the Bradbury's manufactured silver thimbles and perhaps other articles in the jewelry line. The old building next to the Merrill street landing was occupied for many years by Dr. David J. Merrill as a drug store. At some time between 1840 and 1850 Dr. Merrill moved a building near to the upper side of the drug store, which he converted into a house and occupied many years. All the other buildings now standing there have been built in recent years, many of them upon land made by filling up the flats. The passage way to the wharf, now known as White's court, was open after the property came into possession of Dr. D.J. Merrill, the original road to the shipyard, now closed, being several rods above the present court.

Of all the industries that flourished upon or near this territory a century or more ago, the only one now remaining is the distillery owned by the Caldwell's, which was started about 1765, and passed into the hands of Alexander Caldwell about 1772.

O.B. MERRILL

NORTH END PAPERS. NO. 21

Newburyport Daily News, Saturday, February 15, 1908

Congress and Buck Streets.

1800 to 1845

The development that followed the opening of new streets in this locality about the middle of the 18th century, resulted in the erection of a class of houses upon Merrimac street, Merrill lane and Ash lane that with few exceptions were cheap, built by mechanics who wished to live as near the river as possible so as to be near their places of labor. The pleasant locations upon the higher land away from the river were not desired or could not be obtained. The opening of Kent and the new streets above started an interest in real estate that lasted until the time of the war of 1812.

This paper gives an account of the tract of land bounded by Kent, Olive, Congress and Russia streets. In 1800 Olive lane and Kent street ran from Merrimac to High; Ash lane from Merrimac to a fence and Merrill lane from Merrimac to the present Russia street where it turned at a right angle and ran through to Kent street. No other lanes were open in the whole tract of land from Merrimac to High and from Olive to Kent streets.

On the corner of Kent and Russia, then Merrill street, stood an old house owned in 1800 by Peter Gilbert and later by Mr. Coffin. This house was burned and the premises finally sold to Mr. James Woods who places there a carriage shop. Various members of the Merrill family owned and occupied houses in this vicinity. The large house on the upper side of Russia and not far from Merrill street was the residence of Moses Merrill—a man of some prominence a century ago. When Merrill lane was opened it was extended a few rods to reach an old house owned by Thomas Merrill. On the corner of Merrill and Russia and next to Thomas Merrill's stood the house owned by Capt. Joseph Babson and Elisha Gurney. All these houses except that of Thos. P. Merrill are now standing, strong, substantial buildings, good for another century of wear.

Thomas P. Merrill's old house which stood between Capt. Babson's and the modern house on the corner of Congress, and known for many years as Aunt Nabby's was torn down a few years ago.

On the southwest side of these estates was a sunny and beautiful tract of field land reaching to High street. A part of this land from Kent to the head of Merrill lane was owned by Joshua Carter and John Greenleaf; the remainder from Merrill lane to Olive lane by Moses Merrill and Thomas Merrill, Jr. Through this land Congress street was opened—the part from Kent to Merrill about 1805; the remainder to Olive lane about 1811 or 1812. Carter's land was the lower part of the street, inherited from his father Nathaniel in 1799.

The first lot sold was to John Adams in 1806, "on a new street laid out by myself and Greenleaf" says the deed. Upon this lot Adams built the two story house now standing. In 1807 Carter sold to Nathaniel Towle 18 rods for $504 "on a new street from Kent to Merrill lane." In 1807 Carter sold to Eben Gunnisen 12.87 rods for $321.75 on a "continuation of Merrill lane." The street seems to have lacked a name until the church was built when it was called Silk street and afterwards Congress. Why it was given these names is not known. As a name was not then given to Russia street the name of "Merrill" could not have been given the new street unless the change of name of the Russian street was then anticipated.

Towle at once built upon his lot on the corner of Merrill street the large three story house now there, and Gunnison *sic* the three story double house next to Towle. The price paid for these lots and the style of houses built show that this was expected to become a fashionable locality. A very necessary adjunct to a house a century ago was a well, but none was dug here until 1809. Gunnison built his house as an investment and in 1808 sold it to John Patten of Amesbury, brickmaker, for $3000. In 1809 Towle sold Patten a strip of land to include half the well which he and Patten had dug and stoned together.

Patten bought the house to rent but soon tired of it and in 1812 we find the house advertised for sale "on a new street near the new Baptist meeting house, large enough for two large or four small families, with barn, shed and well." In 1815, Towle sold to his brother, Jabez Towle half his house on Silk street for $825. In 1808 Carter sold to Stephen Toppan the lot on the corner of Kent street, 33 rods for $990, and upon this Toppan built the three story house now there which was sold to Hervey Wilber and by him in 1834 to Geo.

Towle. In 1823 this house was taxed to Stephen Toppan and in 1831 to Wilbur for $800. In 1834, it was sold to George Towle for $1075, only $85 more than the land cost in 1808.

The part of Congress from Olive to Merrill street was opened about 1811 or 1812, the first lot sold being for the new Baptist church. In the great fire of 1811 the Baptist church on Liberty street had been burned and the society decided to build a new one on Silk street. Some years later Joseph Alley built a house near the church; the Towle girls a double house on the corner of Merrill and Congress in 1846 and George Towle the house on the corner of Congress and Kent. On the upper side of Congress street stood the old house of Timothy Cutter afterwards occupied by D. Hall Cutter. No other dwelling houses stood on this street until after 1861. The old house on the corner of Congress and Olive was built by Thomas Merrill, Jr. about 1798 or '99. In 1800 he is taxed for an unfinished house value $300, in later years, finished, $1000. It was afterwards owned by Robert Merrill, then by Solomon Scias and in 1832 by Thomas Baker, and finally by John McCusker, whose heirs now own it.

In 1797 Capt. John Buck and T. Woodman bought of the heirs of Cutting Bartlett, two acres of land measuring eight rods on High street, and running 40 rods on the southeast by land of Nathan Hoyt and John Stone. The same year Buck and Woodman divided their purchase. Buck taking the part bordering upon land on Greenleaf and Carter. Buck street was opened by Buck on one side and Greenleaf and the heirs of Carter on the other, probably about 1800. Woodman built upon his "acre" the house now occupied by Nathan Withington, Esq., and Captain Buck erected the large brick house on the corner of High and Buck streets about the year 1800. On the assessors book for 1800 it is taxed unfinished for $900. In 1812 it was assessed for $4500, and in 1821 with about half the land for $1800. In 1812 we find advertised "a lot of land on a new street leading to the new Baptist meeting house from Capt. John Buck's new brick house." Joseph Cutter for $2800 and in 1837 it was owned by Edward Toppan who in 1847 sold it to the wife of John Wills for $3900.

The three story brick house second from the corner of Washington street was built by Simeon Rowell of Amesbury "housewright" who in 1811 bought of Buck 20 rods of land at $40 a rod. Rowell mortgaged the house and in 1814 the mortgage was foreclosed and the house sold to John Morse of Amesbury, who in turn sold it to David Tuxbury. Tuxbury in 1819 sold it to John Pettingell for $800, just what the land cost in 1811. This fall in value was the result of the collapsing of the land boom that began in this part of the town about the beginning of the century, and this depreciation in real estate values continued for more than 20 years through causes that the old town was powerless to withstand.

Mr. Pettingell who at this time owned all of Buck's acre except the part immediately around the brick house on High street, conveyed by his will to his daughter, the wife of Capt. John H. Spring, the brick house bought of Tuxbury. In 1823 this house was assessed for $1000, and in 1832 Spring sold it to Joshua Sanborn for $1100. The following year Sanborn conveyed it to the town of Newburyport, probably to settle tax bills. The town in 1833 sold the property to Capt. Thomas Choate and after his death his heirs sold it in 1845 to Hiram Canney, the well known blacksmith whose gleaming forge shot out its sparks in a shop that stood and now stands on the court on the upper side of the railway embankment. This court was a part of the bridge road when the bridge was a double decker, with the track above and two roadways for teams below. After the new bridge for the railroad was built the entrance to the travel bridge was placed on the lower side, and the old part of the bridge road became Mechanics court.

O.B. MERRILL

NORTH END PAPERS. NO. 22

Newburyport Daily News, Saturday, February 29, 1908

The Field Between Kent and Buck Streets.

Not many houses were built in Newburyport in the 20 years following the beginning of the war of 1812. Few sales of property took place except to settle estates or when the sheriff wound up the affairs of an unlucky trader. Hence the demand for house lots was slight and large tracts of land remained about as the "lott layers" laid them out in the early days of the colony. From Boardman street nearly to Ashland street were large fields measuring from four to 10 or 12 acres, fronting on High street and reaching halfway to the river, a region now thickly covered with houses but upon which in 1830 there were not more than 25 houses nearly all built in the early part of the century.

One such field of about seven acres was between Buck and Kent streets and upon this at the head of Buck street the first modern house at the North End was built. This field was owned in 1681 by Isaac or Isaiah Bayley and no evidence appears to show any earlier owner we conclude that he was the first one. At some time in the next century the whole or a part of it was owned by Jonathan Woodman, grandson of Jonathan, the ship builder. This is shown by a deed dated 1752 in which the sister of Jonathan conveys to Sylvanus Plummer, "land on the corner of Woodman's land and the county road in the upper field." Some years later the lower part of the field of four and a half acres was owned by the Greenleaf family, and the part on High street, about two and a half acres by Nathaniel Carter, who owned more land of this kind than any man at the North End. In 1800 the part of Congress street, was owned by Col. John Greenleaf, and the part of High street by Hannah Smith, of Boston, one of the heirs of Carter. In 1831 this land was for sale. The town authorities being in want of gravel for the roads, on Oct. 1831, the selectmen were authorized "to buy the land on Kent street owned by the late Col. John Greenleaf and now in possession of Daniel Gilman at the sum not exceeding five hundred dollars" says the town book. In Dec. 1831 the selectmen drew an order on the town treasurer for that amount. The land on High street, 420.83 rods, was sold to Hervey Wilbur for $250. These prices are indicative of the financial depreciation of real estate. In 1806-07-08, lots on Congress street sold for $25 and more and on Buck street for $40 a rod, in 1831 the average was about 60 cents. The part used as a gravel pit for more than 20 years was on the upper side of Washington street, and the depression in the rear of the houses there was caused by the removal of gravel.

The first buildings built upon the "Town's Field" were two wooden school houses—the one on the corner of Buck street, now the ward room, built in 1841 for a grammar school for girls, and the other the same year as a primary school for girls on the corner of Kent street. The latter building was moved to Moultonville and serves as a schoolhouse for that part of the city. In 1843 a demand arose for a new engine house for engine No. 3. The old house stood on Kent's landing where it had been located many years. In 1843, the town voted to sell the old house, and build a new one either, "on the center of Kent's Landing or on the town's land on Congress street." The house was built on Congress street, midway between the schoolhouse but when the brick schoolhouse was erected in 1856 the engine house was moved to its present location. In 1882, the wooden engine house having been injured by fire, necessity arose for a new house and in 1883 the present brick house was built at a cost of $4811. In 1861, Washington street was extended to Kent, dividing the "Town's field" into two parts, the land on the lower side of the street being used for public buildings and for a common—the upper part sold for house lots. The town authorities were blamed in 1831 for extravagance in buying this field for $500. The use of it for public purposes for 30 years paid a good interest on its cost, while the sale of house lots has brought many times that sum and the income from taxation of valuable estates there amounts each year to as much as the original cost. Hence the town fathers of 1831 may be acquitted of the charge laid upon them.

While the lower part of this field is historically interesting from its public use, the upper portion on High street is equally interesting as the first modern building upon the whole block was erected there—on the corner of Buck and High Street. This was a combined school house and dwelling, "the Newtonian Institute" intended to be a school of high grade for young ladies. At the time this school opened in 1832, the public schools for girls were kept only in summer and then only for the elementary studies. The Latin Grammar and writing schools had been maintained from 1764 without a break but these were for boys only. There were, however, many private schools taught in general by teachers of marked ability, and in some cases more efficient than the public schools from which the charity idea had not been entirely eliminated. In 1832, the town was financially poor, but its pride was not less than in the palmy days before the embargo, the war and the great fire. This was especially true of its educational interests, in which the reputation of the town was far above the average.

In 1826 the state passed a law giving school committees larger powers than they had before possessed and this act started a movement in educational matters that improved greatly the common school, as it revolutionized the manner of managing them. In a few years the Latin grammar schools became High schools and the old writing schools after passing through the Lancasterian system became the modern grammar schools.

In our own town this change took place several years earlier than in other towns. In the year 1832 the grammar school under Howard and Page became the high school, and the old monitorial writing schools were changing to modern grammar schools, while forces were at work that a few years later caused the grammar schools for girls to be kept the year round, culminating in the establishment of the female high in 1843. It was this condition of things without doubt that led Rev. Hervey Wilbur to open a school that had it been financially supported, would have been superior to any school in town either public or private.

Not the least attractive feature of this school was the building. As nearly all the private schools were kept in halls or in rooms in private houses, their accommodations were inconvenient and unsanitary. The Newburyport Academy building was of course the best as to school purposes. Rev. Hervey Wilbur was educated for the ministry and had charge of a church in Wendall, Mass. He seems to have been more a teacher than a minister and was very successful as a lecturer upon history and natural science, especially astronomy. As he was well furnished with apparatus and diagrams for illustrating his subjects his services were sought not only by the public generally, but by the colleges as well. Mr. Wilber published several books on religious subjects which were well received. Mr. Wilbur came to this town about 1830 and bought of Stephen Toppan the three story house near the corner of Congress and Kent streets. It is said that he had been connected with the famous school at Ipswich were Mary Lyon was a teacher. If so we can imagine whence his idea arose of a similar school in Newburyport.

Directly in front of Mr. Wilbur's residence on Congress street was the large and beautiful tract of land unencumbered with buildings, and when in 1831 an opportunity offered to purchase the most desirable part of this field, Mr. Wilbur secured it as a location for his school. Upon this land on the corner of Buck and High streets he built a large and showy building with great Doric columns in front with large assembly room in the rear and living accommodations in the front. It was a part of his plan to lay out the grounds with care and to make of the whole an attractive institution. Evidently his enthusiasm as a teacher obscured his vision as to financial conditions. We have no means of knowing the cost of the plant but in 1835 it was assessed for $2500, which must have been much less than its cost.

The first notice of the school dignified with the name Newtonian Institute appears in the Herald Feb. 24, 1832 and is as follows:

> *The public are informed that the subscriber expects to open a Seminary in High street, on the second Wednesday in April. The site and style of the buildings to be occupied; the general plan of education to be pursued; with the reasonableness of the terms offered are already so fully before the public as not to require detail here. Intending and hoping to return value received to house who may patronize the institute, it is hoped that a full attendance the first quarter will afford the means of determining whether it can be rightly conducted and fully sustained.*
>
> *Hervey Wilbur*

Evidently the school was opened according to the notice but as no records are at hand to tell us, we do not know the number of students or teachers nor the rates of tuition. In other private schools the tuition was from three to six dollars a term. In 1832 Mr. Wilbur advertised a course of lectures on zoology at the hall of the Newtonian Institute, and the Herald speaks of them as well attended.

The school probably was successful the first year for on March 3, 1833 the prospectus appears in the Herald for the opening of the summer term, in which instruction was to be given in all the English branches;

> ...*in French, Italian, Spanish, Greek and Latin; in the use of the piano-forte, the brush and the needle, charges for board and tuition reasonable; Miss E. Holmes, and other able assistant teachers would be employed. Superior advantages would be received from the lectures to be given with valuable apparatus, Calisthenics and vocal music without extra charge. A branch school would be opened in Pleasant street over Mr. Johnson's store.*

This shows that a wider range of subjects was to be taught and under better conditions than in any schools in town, and gives us a good idea of the sanguine hopes of the able and enthusiastic teacher who put into his scheme his time, talents, energy and money. We find no notice of the school after 1833 and it is probable that soon after the institution closed for want of financial support. The interest on the cost of the plant with running expenses must have been far in excess of the receipts. It was simply a repetition of the experiment that had been tried and failed, of the Newburyport Academy.

We find nothing more about the building until 1836 when it was offered for sale with about a hundred rods of land. It was not sold however, at this time, but some years later was bought by Edward S. Moseley, Esq. After the school was closed the large building was cut in two and the rear part moved a few rods down Buck street where it was converted into a house and sold to a Mr. Colman, a comb maker. Later it was owned by Charles Cheney. The front part of the school building converted into a dwelling was for several years occupied by Mr. Wilbur, until he built the double tenement cottage next above the school building in which he lived, and where he died in 1852. Mr. Wilbur sold for house lots the land upon which two houses were built on High, near the head of Kent street, and two others on Kent street between 1840 and 1850. The school building of the Institute was a few years ago moved from the street corner to give place to a more modern house. It stands now, shorn of its classical features, second from High street. The part of the original building especially used for the school was the two tenement house now third from High on Buck street.

This paper closes the story of the development of the North end of the old town of Newburyport, the territory first owned by Richard Kent, Senior, Edward Woodman and his brother, Archelaus, reaching from North street nearly to Olive and from the river to the middle of High street. The ownership of the upper side of High street from Toppan's lane to Johnson street has not yet been made clear.

I am aware that these papers have not been light reading; they were not intended to be such. Their purpose has been to describe for about two centuries, starting from the first owners of the land, a part of our city never before written about. It has cost a great deal of labor, but I shall feel repaid if it has added even a little to the history of one of the most interesting of the old colonial towns. By the courtesy of the News I have been able to give it to those interested without cost.

O.B. MERRILL

OLIVER B. MERRILL

Newburyport Daily News, May 2, 1912, p 1.

SUDDEN DEATH OF O.B. MERRILL

Was at Work in His Garden this Forenoon When Stricken

His Long Career as School Teacher Endeared Him to Many

Oliver B. Merrill, one of Newburyport's most highly respected citizens and one who has been prominent in its public life, died very suddenly this forenoon of organic disease of the heart.

Mr. Merrill was born in this city where his ancestors here or in the mother town of Newbury, helped to form its history, having settled here early in the 17th century. He was about 75 years of age.

The summons came to Mr. Merrill at 10:45 o'clock at his home on [35] Monroe street. He had been engaged in trimming a grapevine at the rear of his house and feeling ill from the exertion came down the ladder and sat down to rest. Suddenly he sank down and Mrs. Merrill called to a neighbor, M.P. Murphy, who went immediately for medical assistance. He secured Dr. Worcester, but when he reached Mr. Merrill, it was to find that he was past all human aid.

Mr. Merrill had been afflicted with heart trouble for some time and was under medical treatment for it. Yesterday he was down town attending a civil service examination, he being secretary of the local board of examiners.

The deceased was educated in the public schools here, attended Amherst in 1860, and was appointed assistant master at the Brown high school. He was taught school for 30 years, being assistant at the high school when the consolidation was effected.

He resigned in 1892 and retired to private life. He served in the legislature in 1893 and 1894 and from 1895 was a prominent member of the school committee for several years, and because of his educational training he was influential in its affairs.

Much concerning the history of Newburyport and the old parent town has been written by Mr. Merrill, and he has ever taken a deep interest in the public affairs of his native city.

The teachers as well as the public have always entertained a high regard for him and his demise removes a valuable citizen from our midst.

A widow, two sons, Albert A. of Boston, whose home is at Salisbury Point, Prof. William A. of Berkley, Cal., and one daughter Mrs. Herbert Miller of Sandusky, Ohio survive him.

Note by M.P. Motes: Oliver B. Merrill was born 11 January 1836, Newburyport, MA. His wife was Amanda Francis Edgerly, born 11 December 1832 in Gilmanton, NH, died 14 September 1914 in Newburyport. Both are buried in the Belleville Cemetery, Newburyport, MA. They were married 7 November 1858 Stratham, NH.

There children, all born in Newburyport, MA were:
    William Augustus Merrill
    Annie Babson Merrill
    Arthur Robert Merrill
    George Albert Merrill

§§§

Index

A
Abbot
  Butler, 50, 83
Abbott, 90
  Butler, 83, 90
Abbott's tannery, 50
Abel, Capt., 47
Adams, 26
  Archelaus, 3, 15, 16, 20, 21, 23, 25, 27, 28, 30, 65
  John, 16, 30, 31, 102
Adams Field, 26
Adams, Mr., 18
Africa, 53
Agaman, 61
Akerman
  John, 26
  Joseph, 8, 10, 23
  Oliver, 10
Akerman, Mr., 8
Alley
  Joseph, 103
Amburgh
  Van, 23
America, 59, 61
American Machine Co., 78
Amesbury, 69, 102, 103
Amherst College, 111
Anderson
  James, 62
Anderson/Anderton
  James, 83
Anderton/Anderson, 83
  James, 83
Apprentices, 5
Archelaus, 29
Arms Co., 77
Ash Swamp, 81
Ashby
  Wm., 66

Ashby house, 67
Ashe, Mr., 69
Aspen swamp, 82
Assessors book, 94, 95
Atkinson
  Amos, 19
Atkinson, Mr., 78
Atwood
  John, 69
  Thomas, 46, 69
Aunt Hannah, 47
Aunt Nabby, 102

B
Babson
  Joseph, 18
Babson, 3rd
  Joseph, 13
Babson, Capt., 69, 93, 102
  Joseph, 92, 94, 101, 102
Babson, Jr.
  Jos., 34
  Joseph, 14
Babson, Mr., 14
Babylon, 62
Bailey
  John, 83
Baker
  Thomas, 103
Bakery, 78
Balch
  Benj., 33
  Jacob A., 13
  John, 67
  Wm. C., 70
Ballard rifle, 76
Ballard, Mr., 76
Ballou, Mr., 69
Bank
  Institution for Savings, 13, 77
Baptist Church, 103
Baptist meeting house, 103

Bartlett
  Cutting, 103
  Josiah, 84
  Wm., 34
Bass
  Edward, 21, 31
  Bass, Bishop, 16
  Bass, Jr.
    Edward, 16
  Bass, Mr., 16, 17
Bay Colony, 86, 98
Bay of Fundy, 93
Bayley
  Isaac, 87, 88, 105
  Isaiah, 105
Bell, 84
Belleville, 44, 52, 57
Berkley, CA, 112
Bickford
  Horace, 26
Bickford, Esq.
  Horace, 67
Blacksmith, 83
Blacksmith shop, 70, 76
Blake
  Nathan, 12
Blake, Mr.
  Charles W., 83
Blood, 57
  Edwin, 76, 77, 78
  James, 18, 48, 55, 71, 73, 79
Blood grape, 48
Blood, Mr., 48
Bloody Mary, 58
Blue Noses, 93
Boardman, 65
  Nathaniel, 48
Boatbuilder//Joiner, 39, 45, 52, 94
  Choate's joiner shop, 75
  Eben Manson, 75
  Gideon Webster, 75
  Pilsbury, 40, 75
Bond, Dr.
  John, 66

113

Books
 History of
  Newbury, 86
 New England's
  Prospect, 60
Borarus, Capt.
 John, 66
Boston, 8, 23, 53,
  105, 112
Boynton
 Eben Moody, 61
Boys grammer
  school, 19
Bradbury, 89, 95
 Theop. L., 36
 Theophilus, 11
Bradbury, Esq.
 John M., 14
Bradbury, Major
 Ebenezer, 98
Bradbury, Mr., 90
Bradley
 Enoch, 51
Bray, 77
 E.P., 76
Brett
 John, 47, 48
Bridge
 Deer Island, 23,
  52, 55
 Double decker
  bridge, 104
 Essex Merrimac,
  23
 Railroad, 104
Bridge road, 104
Bridges
 Daniel, 17
Brig. *Rapid*, 96
Brithish Army, 93
British Empire, 59
Brook
 Mopan/Mowpan,
  81
Brown, 40, 42
 Alexander, 24
 Charles S., 77
 John, 30, 90

 Moses, 40, 42,
  45, 55, 56,
  69, 75, 94
 Nathan, 84
Brown Square, 17
Brown's wharf, 54
Brown, Capt.
 Eliphalet, 98
 Jacob, 8
Brown, Mr., 76
Brush factory, 78
Buck, 104
Buck, Capt., 103
 John, 103
Builders, 5
Bunker Hill, 47
Buntin
 Thomas, 43
Buntin, Capt.
 Joseph, 43
Buntin, Mr., 8
Burnham
 Jeremiah, 94
Burroughs, 97
 Geo., 49, 56, 97,
  98
 George, 38, 47,
  51
 Rebecca, 38, 39
 Rebecca Kent, 51
 Thomas, 39, 51
Busn, Mr., 71
Buswell
 John, 13
Butler, 95
 John, 83, 95, 97
 Sarah, 95
Button
 Benj., 69
Buzzell
 John, 43

C
Caldwell, 55, 56, 90,
  94, 100
 Alexander, 50,
  55, 63, 87,
  88, 90, 98,
  100

 Moreland, 98
 Wm., 56, 87, 88,
  97
Caldwell Brothers,
  54
Caldwell family, 90
Caldwell's, 94, 100
Caldwell, Sr.
 John, 75
Calendar
 New style, 38
 Old style, 37
California, 90
 Berkley, 112
Call
 A.A., 13
Canney
 Hiram, 104
Carpenter, 5
Carr
 John, 45
Carr's Island, 81
Carr, Brown & Co.,
  45
Carr, Deacon
 John, 45
Carter, 89, 102, 103,
  105
 Jeremiah, 14
 John M., 45
 Nathaniel, 22, 35,
  65, 105
 Thos., 89
Carter's Field, 22, 23,
  25, 31
Carter, Mr, 22, 23
Cartland, 4
Casey
 John, 16
Chace, Capt.
 Bailey, 9
Chandler, 72
 A.D., 9, 72
Chapman
 Henry W., 19
Chase
 James, 48
 Jonathan, 66

114

Cheney
  Charles, 109
  Moses, 65
  Samuel, 46
  William A., 17
Cheney House, 17, 66
Cheney, Capt., 18
  Sarah Gage, 52
  Wm. A., 17
Cheney, Mr., 42
Chickering
  John, 55
Choate, 43
  Benj., 45, 52
  Benjamin, 14, 42
  Ezekiel, 43
  Horace, 79
  True, 42
  William, 39
Choate house, 51
Choate property, 75
Choate, Capt.
  Thomas, 104
Choate, Mr., 67
Churches
  Amenian chapel, 10
  Baptist, 103
  Baptist meeting house, 94, 103
  Hollis Street, 8
  Whitefield, 45
Clark
  Thos., 45
  Weston, 24
Coaster
  Theophilas, 97
Coffin, 40, 42, 56, 98
  Ben., 65
  Benjamin, 97
  David, 42, 46, 65, 66
  Emory, 10, 45
  Joshua, 62, 86
  Moses, 5, 10, 11, 17, 43, 44
  Nathan, 10, 11, 43
  Sam, 56, 97
  Samuel, 47, 56, 98
  Wm., 55
Coffin house, 11
Coffin, Col.
  Fred., 70
Coffin, Dr.
  Chas., 45
Coffin, Major, 33
  David, 33
Coffin, Mr., 47, 83, 101
Coffin, Mrs., 83
Cogswell
  Edward, 52
Coker, 8, 17, 34, 40, 54
  Sam, 19
  Samuel, 16
  Thomas, 3, 4, 5, 7, 10, 16, 19, 20, 34, 65
  Thos., 33, 45
Coleman's Wharf, 44
Coleman, Mr., 20
Collar Company, 79
College
  Hobart Free, 9
Collier, 49
Colman
  Wm., 12
Colman, Mr., 109
Comb makers
  Carr, Brown & Co., 45
Contractors, 5
Coolidge
  M.S., 84
Cooper
  David, 83
Cordage plant, 73
Corliss, 51
  John, 51
Cotton industry, 69
Crafts
  Joe, 11
Creasey
  Sam., 94
  Wm., 48
Creasy
  Francis, 94
Creeden's store, 37, 82
Creeden, Mr., 51, 82
Creedon
  John, 49
Cressey
  Michael, 9
Cressey, Mr., 10
Cromwell, 59
Cross, 44, 56, 90, 97, 98
  Benj., 43
  Mary, 83, 90
  Ruth, 83, 90
  Stephen, 33
  William, 89
  Wm., 83, 89, 90, 97
Cross, Jr.
  Ralph, 89, 92, 97
Cross, Maj.
  William, 89
Cross, Major, 83, 95
  William, 89
Cross, Major., 83
Cross, Sr.
  Wm., 90
Cumnock, Mr., 71
Currency
  New England, 98
Currer, Mr., 98
Currier
  Albert, 26, 46, 65, 70
  Geo., 10
  Solomon, 89
Currier, Mr., 27, 34, 35, 69, 73, 77, 86, 98
Curtis
  Sam, 94
Curtis Hat Factory, 78

115

Cushing
   William, 78
Custom House, 83, 89
Cutter
   D. Hall, 103
   Joseph, 103
   Thomas, 69
   Timothy, 103

D
Daggett
   Nathan, 44
Davis, 95
   Moses, 83
Deer Island, 52
DeFord, 90
Dennet, Mr., 72
Dennis
   James, 49
Depreciated
      currency, 97
Depreciation in real
      estate, 104
Dickens, Dr.
   Job T., 20
Dimmick, Mr., 65
Distiller, 10
Distilleries, 50, 53, 54, 55, 56, 86, 87, 97, 98
   Caldwells, 90
Dockham
   Warren, 76
Dockum
   John, 25
   Joseph, 24
Dodge, 94
   Nathaniel, 45
   Wm. L., 83
Dodge, Mr., 20
Dole, Dr., 99
Donahue, Mr., 96
Double decker
      bridge, 104
Dow
   Timothy, 43
Downes, Mrs., 45

Downing
   Frank, 25
   Joseph, 30
Dresser, Mr., 78
Drown
   Richard W., 13
Drug Store, 99
Duinoussay
   Augustus, 54
   Louis, 54

E
Easkell
   Dan, 84
Edgerly
   Amanda Francis, 82
   David, 18
Edwards
   Edward, 84
   Joseph, 10
   Leroy, 25
Edwards lot, 10
Edwards,
   Edward, 84
Edwards, Mr., 25
   Leroy, 25, 31
Eldorado, 90
Embargo, 93, 107
Emerson
   Samuel, 48
Emery
   Flavins, 19
   Thomas, 19, 32
Emery, Miss, 13
Emery, Rev., 18, 19
Engine Company
   The Warren
      Currier, 10
Engine house, 67, 84, 106
England, 41, 58, 59
English, 93
English
   manufacturer, 73
Essex Deeds, 31
Essex Registry of
   Deeds, 29, 30

Europe, 10, 94
Evans
   W.O., 45
   Winthrop O., 45
Ewing
   John, 84

F
Factory
   Also see Mills
   American
      Machine Co., 78
   Arms Co., 77
   Box factory, 79
   Brush Factory, 78
   Collar Company, 79
   Curtis Hat
      Factory, 78
   Distillery, 50
      (also see
      Distilleries)
   Essex Hat Co., 78
   Globe Mill, 70
   Merrimac Arms
      and Manufac.
      Co., 76
   Sash and Blind, 18
   Shoe factory, 73, 79
   Silver factory, 75, 76
   Tannery, 50
   Towle Manuf..
      Co., 77, 78
Falls River, 73
Fire of 1811, 103
Firearms
   Ballard rifle, 77
   Van Colt, 77
Flanagan, Mr., 25
Flanders
   A.S., 19
Florence, [Italy], 10
Foster, widow, 83
Fowler
   Richard, 26

France, 54, 64, 98
Francis
   Converse, 18, 43
Frazier, Capt., 3
Freeman
   Wm., 43
French, 93
   E.G., 84
Frothingham
   James, 26

G
Gage
   Sarah, 52
Gage house, 52
   Jonathan, 52
Gage, Capt., 52
Gardner
   Geo., 71
   John, 71
George house, 20
Germantown, 47
Gilbert
   Peter, 83, 101
Gilman
   Arthur, 8
   Daniel, 105
Gloucester, MA, 93
Gold rush, 90
Gomn
   Emery, 70
   Fred., 70
Goodrich, Capt.
   Moses, 7
Goodwin
   John, 12
Grasshopper Plains, 79
Gravel for roads, 106
Gravel pit, 106
Graves, 77
Graves, Capt.
   Wm., 77
Gray, Jr.
   Wm., 72
Great Britain, 64
Great Fire, 107
Greaton
   O.W., 25

Obed W., 43, 57
Greeley
   Horace, 11
Green
   Stephen, 10, 72
Greenleaf, 102, 103, 105
   John, 105
Greenleaf family, 105
Greenleaf, Capt., 4, 7
   Jacob, 3
   John, 65
Greenough, 51, 95
Griffin, Esq.
   Ellphalet, 14
Gunnisen
   Eben, 102
Gurney
   Elisha, 93, 101, 102
Gurney, Hon.
   Orrin J., 25, 31

H
Hale
   Jacob, 69
   Moses, 34
Hale, Dr., 9
Hale, Mrs.
   Sarah W., 76
Hale, Rev.
   Benjamin, 9
Haley
   Humphrey, 25
Hart
   James, 43
Harvey
   Robert, 84
Haskell, Mr., 83
Haverhill, 87, 88
Hazen
   John P., 94
Heath
   Moody, 17
Hennessey
   Philip, 25
Herald, 8
Hercules, 28, 29

Hills
   Nathaniel, 52
Holker, Mr., 24
Horton
   Daniel, 36
House
   Abel Kents, 83
   Babson, 102
   Boarding house, 71
   Bradbury, 98
   Buck, 103
   Burnham, 94
   Cheney, 17, 66
   Choate, 51
   Coffin, 98
   Coffin, Mrs., 83
   Cross, 89
   Foster, 83
   George, 20
   Kent, 61, 86
   Keyes, 65, 71
   Kingsbury, 89
   Market, 9, 14
   Merrill, 92, 102
   Papanti, 10, 14
   Pike, 92
   Sanborn, 93
   Sawyers, 25, 49, 82
   Somerby, 82
   Somerby, Mrs., 82
   Still, 97
   Tenement, 77, 109
   Three story, 83
   Titcomb, 86
   Toppan, 90
   Tuxbury, 104
   Waterman, 69
   Williams, 51, 78
   Woodland Cottage, 76
   Woodman's, 87
House of Entertainment, 52

House of
    Representatives, 43
Hovey, Capt., 39
Howe, Dr., 26
Hoyt
    John, 39
    Nathan, 103
Hoyt, Capt., 44
    Joseph, 25
Hubbard
    Edward, 30
Hunt
    Hugh, 30
Hurd, Dr., 67
Huse
    Wm. H., 43, 92

I
Indians, 61
Ingalls, Mr., 67
Institution for
    Savings, 77
Ipswich registry, 86, 87
Ipswich, MA, 107
Ireland, 64

J
Jackman
    Geo. L., 13
Jackson
    Charles, 33
Jackson, Judge
    Charles, 3
Jail, 93
Jefferson's gunboat, 93
Jefferson, President
    Thomas, 93
Jeweler, 7
Johnson, 110
Johnson's Head, 13
Johnson, Capt.
    Wm. P., 9
Johnson, Dr., 13
Jones, Capt.
    Reuben, 20
Juteau
    Jolin, 55

K
Kent, 49, 60, 62, 86, 87
    Abel, 37, 38, 40, 44, 82, 83
    Benj., 40
    Goodman, 60, 61, 62
    John, 32, 39, 49, 50, 62, 75, 83, 92
    Joshua, 36, 43
    Joshua, son of John, 47
    Mary, 39
    Rebecca, 51, 89
    Richard, 32, 37, 38, 39, 40, 49, 50, 51, 56, 59, 62, 81, 86, 92
Kent family, 40
Kent Field North, 42
Kent house, 61
Kent land, 46
Kent Street, 81
Kent's house, 61
Kent's landing, 49, 50, 53, 56, 57, 81, 87, 88, 96, 106
Kent, Abel, 36
Kent, Capt
    John, 89, 96
Kent, Dea.
    John, 81
Kent, Deacon
    John, 32, 37, 47, 50, 54, 55, 81
Kent, Joshua, 36
Kent, Jr.
    Richard, 58
Kent, Mariner, 36, 38, 40, 42, 46
Kent, Sr.
    Goodman
        Richard, 63

    Richard, 33, 36, 50, 58, 75, 82, 109, 110
Kents landing, 96
Keyes
    Abel, 25
Keyes house, 65, 71
Kimball, Mr., 7, 8, 43
King Charles, 29
King Charles II, 99
Kingsbury, 89
    Benjamin, 51
    Henry, 50, 89, 97
    John, 89, 97
    Rebecca, 89
    Rebecca Kent, 89
Knight
    John, 56, 98
Knowlton
    Joanna, spinster, 97

L
Lady Anne, 64
Lancasterian system, 107
Landings, 98
Lanes
    Dove, 49
    Goodwin's, 34
    Moody's, 31, 33, 49
    Toppan, 64
    Toppan's, 20
    Woodman, 1
    Woodman's, 31, 32, 33, 37, 64
Lawrence, 69
Leach
    Hiram, 43, 44
Leonard, Dr.
    Wm. B., 84
Lesley
    Edward S., 70
Lesley, Mr., 71
Leslie, 70
    Edward S., 71
Lewis
    Moses, 65

Liquor
 Distilled, 53
Little
 Edward, 20
 Josiah, 51
 M.C., 93
 Moses, 54
 Little and Young, 54
Little, Esq.
 Isaac, 28
Littlefield, 54, 56, 57
 Solomon, 98
Littlefield, Mr., 99
London, 28, 59
Lord
 John B., 18
Lott Layers, 82, 105
Lovejoy
 Charles, 25
Lowell, 69
Lunt
 E.A., 84
Lynn, 61
Lyon
 Mary, 107

M
Mace
 Ab., 84
 Wm., 43
Maine, 44
Mall, 84
Manufacturer
 Bradbury, 99
March
 Eben, 36
Market House, 9, 14
Market Square, 13,
  24, 44, 49,
  81, 99
Marsh
 Angier, 13
 Geo., 64
Maryland, 54
Mason
 Jona, 38
 Jonathan, 83
 Wm. Toppan, 83
Massachusetts

Newburyport, 82
Massachusetts
 colony, 59
Massachusetts
 Company,
 58, 60
Massachusetts
 soldiers, 48
McCusker
 John, 103
McLean, Assistant
 Marshall
 John, 25
McLean, Marshall
 John, 25, 31
Mead, 44
Medford rum, 53
Mercer, 28
Mercer of Malford,
 28
Merimack River, 1
Merrill, 77, 95
 Albert, 112
 Amanda Francis
  Edgerly, 82
 Annie Babson, 82
 Arthur Robert, 82
 Aunt Hannah, 49
 Dan., 48
 David J., 92
 Enoch, 9
 Geo., 76
 George Albert,
  82
 Henry, 39, 96
 James, 17, 95
 Jas., 48
 Jonathan, 51, 55
 Luther, 75
 Moses, 92, 101,
  102
 O.B., 25
 Oliver B., 1, 111
 P.A., 17
 Robert, 103
 Robert M., 14
 Thomas, 49, 101
 Thomas P., 102
 Thos., 38, 94

Thos. P., 92, 94,
 101
William
 Augustus, 82
Merrill family, 101
Merrill, Dr.
 D.J., 100
 David J., 99
Merrill, Jr.
 Henry, 39, 50
 Thomas, 103
Merrill, Mr.
 Henry, 77
Merrill, Mrs., 111
Merrill, Prof.
 William A., 112
Merrill, Sr.
 Henry, 39
Merrilll & Savier, 56
Merrimac, 60, 82, 86
Merrimac Arms &
  Manufacturin
  g Co., 76
Merrimac River, 87,
 95, 96
Merrimac Valley, 4
Merrimack, 87
Merrow, Mr.
 James, 69
Merwin, Mr., 76
Middleton
 Wm., 48
Milbury
 Wm., 52
Militia, 89
Miller, Mrs.
 Herbert, 112
Millikin
 Seth, 72
Mills
 Also see Factories
 Bartlett, 69, 70,
  73, 80
 Essex, 73
 Globe, 70, 73
 James, 70, 73
 Ocean, 9, 18, 26,
  46, 67, 68,

119

69, 70, 71, 72, 73, 78
Whitefield Co., 10, 72, 73
Miltiman
   John, 63
Miltmore
   John, 50
Milton
   C.W., 84
Molasses, 53
Montgomery, 65
Moody, 32, 33
Moody's land, 32, 51, 92
Moore, Mr., 92
Mopan/Mowpan, 81
Moreland, 98
   Wm., 97
Morland
   Wm., 56
Morrill
   Green, 25
Morrison, Capt., 83
Morse
   Goody, 99
   John, 104
   John, of Amesbury, 103
   Jos. B., 71
   Joshua, 18
   Wm., 52
Morse', Mrs., 99
Morse, Mrs., 70
Morse, Rev. James, 70
Moseley, Esq. Edward S., 109
Moulton, 89
   H.W., 77
   Henry W., 76
   N.A., 92
   Richard W., 13
   Wm., 88
Moulton, Miss S.J., 84
Moultonville, 106
Murphy M.P., 111

N
National Biscuit Co., 69
Nesbit
   Hannah Woodman, 94
   Hannah, dau of Jonathan, 94
New England, 11, 73, 79
New Hampshire, 18
   Gilmanton, 82
New York, 72
Newbury, 1, 4, 20, 22, 23, 27, 28, 29, 30, 33, 59, 61, 81, 86, 87, 111
Newbury settlers, 58
Newburyport, 1, 18, 22, 23, 53, 80, 82, 86, 93, 105, 111
Newburyport Academy, 5, 107
Newburyport Daily News, 1
Newburyport Herald, 76
Newell
   Joseph, 9
Newell, Capt., 47
Newspaper
   Herald, 12, 13, 20, 44, 55, 66, 78, 108
   Newburyport Daily News, 3, 7
   Newburyport Herald, 76
Newtonian Institute, 67, 106, 108
Nichols

Andrew, 54, 55
North boundary, 89
North End, 1, 4, 5, 13, 14, 18, 19, 23, 26, 56, 64, 69, 73, 75, 77, 78
North End Factories, 80
North End Paper, 47
Northwestrn Territory, 11
Norton
   Michael, 48, 49
Noyes
   Cutting, 97
Number of lotts, 96

O
O'Neil, Mr., 18
O'Neill building, 94
Occupations
   Agent, 70, 72
   Apprentices, 5
   Beer manufacturing, 62
   Blacksmith, 70, 76, 83, 104
   Boat building, 57
   Boatbuilder, 40, 75
   Book trade, 13
   Brickmaker, 102
   Builder, 5, 87, 88, 98
   Butcher, 9, 83
   Cabinet maker, 47
   Cabinet making, 12
   Carpenter, 5, 26, 70
   Coaster, 97
   Collector, 89
   Comb maker, 109
   Comb makers, 109
   Contractors, 5

Cordwainer, 43, 44
Custom house officers, 29
Dealer in swine, 8
Deputy collector, 89
Distilled liquor, 53
Distiller, 10, 17
Glazier, 90
Grocer, 16, 43
House of Entertainment, 52
House Painting, 66
Housewright, 103
Jeweler, 7, 13, 16, 43
Joiner, 75, 94, 97
Judge, 8
Leather dresser, 83
Loom builder, 70
Lott layers, 27, 105
Machine shop, 24
Machinist, 70
Maltser, 62
Manager, 72, 76
Manufacturer, 99
Mariner, 89, 97
Mason, 70
Mason worker, 94
Master, 99
Mechanic, 52, 76
Mechanics, 95
Merchant, 50, 83, 98
Naval officer, 89
Organ builder, 47
Peddler, 19
School marm, 47
School master, 84
Seamen, 94

Sheriff, 105
Ship builder, 52, 96, 97, 98, 103, 105
Ship joiner, 39, 45, 52, 94
Shipper, 98
Shipwright, 89, 97
Shoemaker, 43
Soap boiler, 17
Surveyor, 35, 83, 89, 90
Tailor, 43
Tanner, 50, 83
Teacher, 84, 106, 108
Teamster, 98
Watchmaker, 43
Wool puller, 83
Ohio, 11
Sandusky, 112
Ordway
  Parsons, 69
Orne
  John, 38
  Wm., 90
  Orne, Capt., 38
  Wm., 83
  Orne, Wm., 90
Osgood
  Samuel, 42
  Timothy, 42

P
Page, 95
Palmer
  Timothy, 33
Papanti, 19, 23, 24, 26
  "Signor", 10, 14, 19
  Lorenzo, 10
Papanti house, 14
Paper collars, 78
Papinti, Mr., 11
Parker River, 60
Parochial School, 19
Patch, Capt.

Joseph, 49
Patten
  Ellza, 26
  Herbert, 14
  John of Amesbury, 102
Payne, Deacon
  Henry, 24
Payne, Mr., 24
Pearce's farm, 50
Pearson
  Benj., 84
  Benjamin, son of John, 38
  Charles, 83
  Geo., 82
  John, 42
  Michael, 51, 76, 78
  Simeon, 84
  Stephen, son of John, 38
Pearson, Deacon, 47
  Charles, 50
  John, 36, 38, 46
Pearson, Mr., 36
  John F., 25, 31
Petingill
  Abigail, 38
Pettingell, 26
  John, 4, 103
Pettingell, Mr., 104
Pettingill
  John, 36
Philbrick, Mr., 7
Phillsbury, 39
Pickett
  Ben., 52
  Wm., 94
Pickett, Capt.
  Joseph, 93, 94
Pidgeon, 94
  Benj., 95
Pierce
  Jacob M., 13
Pierpoint
  John, 8

Pike
  Benj., 91
  Benjamin, 19
  Daniel, 91
  John D., 79
  John N., 77
  Richard, 65, 66
  Stephen, 46
Pike's land, 91
Pike, Elder
  D.P., 19
Pilbrick, Mr., 71
Pillsbury, 3rd
  Sam, 39, 45
Pilsbury, 40, 86
  Alfred, 39
  Benjamin, 45
  John, 45
  Mary, 38
  Moses, 28
  Sam, 40
  Samuel, 36
  Stephen, 52
Pilsbury house, 33
Pilsbury, 3rd
  Samuel, 36
Plains, The, 28
Plumer
  Nath., 84
  Richard, 24
  Sylvanus, 65, 66
Plummer
  Nathan, 94
  Sylvanus, 105
Poore, 81
  Joseph, 28
  Sam, 28
Popkins
  Wm., 84
Porter
  Wm., 94
Prince
  James, 89
Privateer
  Salisbury, 93
Puritan, 29

Q
Queen Elizabeth, 58
Quill
  Daniel, 18
Quimby, 94
  Moses, 67

R
Railroad, 37, 104
Railroad depot, 26
Rawson, Mr., 60
Read, Mr., 78
Real estate
  depreciation,
  104, 106
Reed
  E.M., 75, 76
  James, 26
Reed, Mr., 76
  Enoch M., 9
Revolutionary War
  Soldier, 48
Revolution, 47, 59
Revolutionary men,
  48, 89
Richards
  Dan, 75
Richardson
  Daniel, 51
  Pottle, 18, 52
Ridge, the, 81
Rimick
  Joseph, 54
Ring
  Robert, 62
River, 39, 68, 86
  Artichoke, 27
  Merrimac, 27, 36,
    61, 87
  Natural highway,
    96
  Parker, 27, 58, 60
River lots, 97
River Lotts, 96
Roads
  Bridge, 54, 56
  Curson's mill, 28
  River, 55
  Turkey Hill, 10

Roberts
  Parker, 43
Roberts, Mr., 44
Rogers
  Geo., 84
Rogers, Mr., 26
Rolf
  Sam, 56
Rollins
  Samuel, 49
Rowell, 51
  Joseph, 64
  Simeon, 103
  Simeon, of
    Amesbury,
    103
Rubbish, 50
Rum, 53, 97, 98
Russia, 94

S
Salem, 1, 30, 33
Salisbury, 30, 93, 112
Salisbury Point, 93
Sanborn
  Gabez, 93
  Joshua, 104
Sanderson, Miss, 47
Sandusky, OH, 112
Sargent, 57
  Charles R., 12
  Elbridge, 51
  True, 51
Saunders
  Ben., 70
  Benj., 71
Savage, Dr., 28, 29
Sawyer, 44, 45
  A.H., 4
  Albert, 25
  Jeremiah, 12, 44
  Josiah, 69
Sawyer house, 25
Sawyer's house, 31
Sawyer, Mrs., 82
Sayers
  Robert, 59
School house, 10, 22,
  67, 83, 84

Schools
  Amherst College, 111
  Boys grammar school, 19
  Brick school house, 84
  Brown High School, 111
  Dames, 84
  For dames, 84
  Girls Grammar School, 84
  Girls school, 106
  Grammar schools, 84
  High schools, 107
  Jackman School, 23
  Kelly School, 23
  Lancasterian system, 107
  Latin Grammar school, 106
  Latin grammer school, 22
  Latin Grammer school, 106
  Latin grammer school, 107
  At the Mall, 84
  Moultonville, 106
  Newburyport Academy, 5, 107
  Newtonian Institute, 106, 108
  North, 67
  North male grammar school, 84
  North School, 23
  Parochial School, 18
  Private, 84, 108
  School for boys, 84
  School house, 84
  Schoolhouse, 82
  Schools for girls, 84
  Seminary, 108
  On Town's Field, 106
  Writing schools, 84, 107
Scias
  Solomon, 103
Scotsman, 71
Searle
  George, 52
Selfridge, Mr., 26
Servier, Capt, 84
Sevier Girls, 51, 83
Sevier, Capt., 51, 84
  Joseph, 51, 55, 83
Sewall, 86
  Henry, 87
  John, 28
Sewall, Jr.
  Henry, 97
Sewall, Master, 22, 87
  Henry, 86
Shaw
  Sam, 84
Ships
  Brig. *Rapid*, 96
  John and Mary, 59
  Salamanda, 96
  Salamander, 98
  Schooner *The Dove*, 39
  Schooner *Sally*, 94
Shipyard, 87, 88, 96, 97, 100
  Cross, 95
  Merrill, 96
  Merrill's, 97
  Woodmans, 89
Shoe factory, 73, 79

Shop, 83
Shops
  Blacksmith, 76
  Brass foundry, 78
  Carpenter, 78
  Carpenters, 50
  Distillery, 78
  Drug store, 78
  Grocery, 57, 75, 78
  Joiner shop, 75
  Machine shop, 24
  Meat, 78
  Paint shop, 69
  Stove shop, 69
  Tavern, 52
  Silver factory, 81
  Silver thimbles, 99
Skeels
  Amos, 17
Slaughter house, 10
Smart
  Harrison, 67
Smith
  Hannah, of Boston, 105
  Hannan, of Boston, 105
  Josiah, 65
  Michael, 50, 83
  Nathaniel, 20
  Wm., 65
Smith, Mr., 23
Smithfield, 58
Society
  Marine, 9
Somerby, 36
  Anthony, 23
  Joseph, 35, 54
  Somerby house, 49
  Somerby, Capt. Abram, 69
  Somerby, Mr., 35
Southhampton, 28
Southwick
  Henry, 7
  James, 7
Spalding/Spaulding
  Jeptha, 52

Oliver, 43
Sprague, 56
    Joseph, 55
Spring
    John H., 71
Spring, Capt.
    John, 104
    John H., 4
Spring, Mr.
    John R., 8
State house, 98
Stedman
    Ebenezer, 13
Stickney
    Eben, 36
    Jonathan, 48
Still house, 97
Stockman
    R., 48
Stone
    John, 103
    Richard, 52
    Richard W., 13
Stores
    Chesley &
        Merrill, 75
    Creeden's store,
        37, 75, 82
    Donahue, Mr., 96
    Drug store, 99
    Grocery, 9, 43, 99
    Johnson's, 109
    Mr. Johnsons, 109
    Mr. Sargents, 75
Storey, 52
Stratton
    Bartholnew, 98
    Bartholomew, 99
Streets/Lanes
    Ash lane, 94, 95, 96, 101
    Ashland, 81, 105
    Birch, 35
    Boardman, 17, 67, 105
    Broad, 3, 4, 5, 7, 8, 9, 10, 11,

12, 24, 25, 32, 33, 34, 35, 39, 40, 41, 42, 43, 44, 45, 66, 69, 71, 75, 76, 77, 81
    Buck, 23, 67, 85, 103, 105, 106, 108, 109
    Calculation, 36
    Caldwell court, 89
    Carter, 11, 18, 19, 23, 24, 25, 26, 36, 42, 46, 47, 53, 54, 56, 62, 64, 65, 66, 67, 70, 74, 103
    Charles, 70
    Congress, 67, 82, 85, 86, 92, 101, 102, 103, 105, 106, 107
    Court, 13
    Curson Mill Road, 28
    Cutter's Court, 25
    Dove, 36, 38, 39, 47, 49, 69
    Eagle, 10, 26, 65, 66, 67, 70, 74
    Elm, 91, 94, 95
    Essex, 35
    Federal, 70
    Forrester, 19
    Green, 36, 52, 53, 56
    Greenleaf, 103
    Harris, 35
    High, 3, 11, 12, 13, 14, 18, 19, 20, 23, 24, 27, 32, 34, 36, 64, 65, 66, 67,

68, 69, 81, 87, 88, 101, 102, 103, 104, 105, 106, 108, 109, 110
Jefferson, 34
Johnson, 109, 110
Kent, 1, 6, 28, 32, 34, 38, 47, 51, 53, 54, 55, 58, 59, 60, 62, 63, 64, 65, 66, 67, 68, 69, 70, 72, 74, 75, 81, 82, 83, 84, 87, 88, 94, 101, 102, 103, 105, 107, 109
Kent Street building, 84
Keyes, 65
Lafayette court, 26
Liberty, 43, 94, 103
Lloyd, 65, 70
Low, 10, 15, 27
Lower, 27
Market, 32, 36, 89, 99
Market Square, 81
Mechanics Court, 104
Merrill, 89, 90, 91, 92, 93, 94, 96, 99, 101, 102, 103
Merrill lane, 88
Merrimac, 16, 23, 27, 32, 33, 34, 36, 37, 38, 39, 40, 42, 43, 44, 46, 47, 49,

50, 54, 55, 56, 60, 65, 69, 70, 71, 75, 76, 77, 79, 81, 82, 83, 88, 89, 90, 91, 92, 93, 94, 97, 98, 101
Merrimac Court, 81
Middle, 15
Monroe, 3, 10, 11, 14, 18, 19, 24, 25, 36, 48, 62, 64, 65, 66, 67, 69, 70, 71, 73, 87, 88, 111
Moody's lane, 81
Mr. Woodman's lane, 87, 88
New Street, 34, 87
North, 1, 6, 15, 16, 18, 19, 20, 22, 23, 32, 33, 35, 36, 37, 39, 40, 41, 45, 47, 49, 50, 60, 63, 67, 69, 109, 110
North Atkinson, 43, 57
Oakland, 1, 43, 50, 68, 75
Ocean, 25, 70, 72, 74
Olive, 50, 67, 81, 86, 87, 93, 101, 103, 109, 110
Oliver, 62
Pleasant, 8, 35, 52, 69, 70, 109
Poore's lane, 81

Private, 106
Russia, 82, 83, 84, 92, 93, 94, 101, 102
School, 22
Silk, 102, 103
South Green, 96
State, 8, 12, 43
Toppan, 27, 87
Toppan's lane, 27, 28, 82, 86, 110
Turkey Hill, 15
Tyng, 3, 9, 11, 12, 13, 14, 16, 17, 18, 19, 20, 22, 32, 33, 34, 35, 36, 40, 42, 45, 66, 67, 69, 75, 81
Walnut, 34
Warren, 26, 32, 34, 36, 38, 45, 47, 48, 65, 66, 70, 72, 79
Washington, 20, 26, 54, 67, 103, 106
White's court, 100
Whites court, 99
Winter, 22, 54, 71
Woodland, 13, 57, 81
Woodman, 32, 92
Woodmans lane, 81, 82, 86, 87, 88, 89, 90, 92, 96, 97
Striped Pig, 53
Swain
  Levi, 65, 66
Swamp
  Ash, 81
  Aspen, 82
Swasey, Mr., 7

Wm. H., 8
Swett
  Ellen, 84

T
Tappan
  Mary, 84
Tavern, 52
  Deer Island, 52
Teel
  Babson, 18
  Seth, 18
  Wm., 18
Tenement, 109
Tewkesbury
  John, 57
Thomas, 9, 13, 14, 34, 40
Thomas, 3, 33, 54, 55
Thomas & Whipple, 13
Titcomb, 87
  E., 84
  Geo., 84
  Joshua, 56
  Paul, 12
  Priscilla, 84
  Wm., 62
Titcomb, Mr., 86, 87, 88
Titcombs, 86
Toll house, 5, 52
Toothbrushes, 78
Toppan, 82, 86, 87, 110
  Abner, 12
  Edward, 103
  Eliza, 90
  Enoch, 66
  Jacob, 27, 86, 87
  Moses, 10
  Sam, 91
  Sam., 91
  Sarah, 90
  Stephen, 3, 5, 13, 20, 34, 66, 102, 103, 107
  Wm., 83, 84, 90

Toppan, Lieut.
   Jacob, 28
Torrey
   Nath., 48
Tower bell, 84
Towle, 102
   Geo., 103
   George, 50, 103
   Jabez, 102
   Nath, 94
   Nath., 94
Towle Manufacturing
   Co., 77, 78
Town Field, 106
Tracy, 40
   John, 3, 65
   Nathaniel, 54
   Patrick, 3, 35, 55, 56, 75
Tracy Estate, 12
Tracy Field, 3, 7, 10, 11, 12, 14, 15, 16
Tracy land, 32
Tucker, Mr., 71
   Wm., 14
Tufts
   John, 83, 84
Turkey Hill, 82
Turnpike
   Corporation, 5
Tuxbury, 104
   David, 103
Tyng, 35, 40
   D.A., 33
   Dudley A., 20, 34

U
Uncle Sam, 9
United States [Govt.], 77
Upper Long wharf, 98

V
Van Amburgh
   menagerie, 23
Van Colt, 77

Vinal, Master, 22
Virgin Queen, 58

W
War of 1812, 93, 101
Ward 6, 84
Warren, 48
Waterhouse, 17
Waterman, 40, 42, 45
   Luther, 12, 40
Waterman house, 69
Wattlos
   Joseph, 72
Wead, Mr., 44
Weather Vane
   Quill, 84
Weaver
   Sam Plumer, 97
Webster
   Humphrey, 13, 34
Wendall, Mass, 107
West India Goods, 57
West India Islands, 93
West Indies, 53
West Newbury, 4, 9, 26
West Parish, 28
Wharf,/s 51, 55, 56, 69, 76, 97, 98, 100
   Brown's, 54
   Coleman's, 44
   Upper Long Wharf, 98
Wharf stores, 98
Wheeler
   H., 84
Wheeries, 75
Whig party, 43
White, Esq.
   D.A., 8
Whitefield Church, 45
Whiting
   Jos., 48
   Joseph, 48
Whitmore

Amos, 7
Whitmore, Mr., 7
Whitney
   James, 16
Whitney, Mr., 17
Wilber
   Hervey, 103
Wilbur, 103
   Hervey, 102, 106, 108
   Parson, 67
Wilbur, Mr., 108, 109
Wilbur, Rev.
   Hervey, 107
William
   Mary, 89
   Ruth, 89
Williams
   Abraham, 55
   Abraham & Wm. C., 55
   Joseph, 51, 55, 78, 84
Williams family, 54
Williams house, 51, 78
Williams, Jr.
   Joseph, 56
Williams, Major, 89
Williams, Mrs., 55
Wills
   John, 103
Witchcraft, 99
Witham, Capt., 92
Withington
   Nathan, 103
Wood, 61
   Albert, 66
   David, 66
   William, 60
Wood, 2nd
   David, 66
Wood, Mr., 43
Woodland cottage, 76
Woodman, 29, 31, 83, 103
   Abigail, 64

Abigail, spinster, 97
Amos, 43
Archelaus, 21, 27, 28, 29, 36, 64, 82, 86, 87, 109, 110
Edward, 27, 28, 64, 82, 86, 91, 94, 109, 110
Eliz., 94
Elizabeth, 91, 94
Hannah, 94
Hannah, dau of Jonathan, 94
Henry, 89
Hilton, 64
Ichabod, 87, 89, 91, 92, 94, 97
Ichabod, son of Jonathan, 88, 94, 96
Jonathan, 50, 64, 86, 87, 88, 89, 91, 94, 97, 98, 99, 105
Jonathan, grandson of Jonathan, 105
Lewis, 87
Lewis, son of Ichabod, 88
Moses, 92
Sarah, 65
T., 103
William, 64
Woodman's farm, 86, 88
Woodman's land, 51
Woodman's lane, 75, 81, 87
Woodman's shipyard, 89
Woodman, Lieut. Archelaus, 28
Woodman, Mr., 30, 86, 87, 88, 99
Edward, 62
Woodman, Mrs., 91
widow of Ichabod, son of Jonathan, 91
Woodman, widow of Ichabod, 91
Woods
James, 101
John, 16
Worcester, 76
Worcester, Dr., 111
Wyatt
Benj., 56

Y
York, Mr., 18
Young
Beniah, 54
Young & Little, 78

127